MAKARIOS:
FAITH AND POWER

This work is dedicated to all men and women of goodwill, both Cypriot and British, who have responded to the challenge of difficult times.

MAKARIOS:
FAITH AND POWER

Dr. P. N. VANEZIS

Introduction by James Cameron

Abelard-Schuman Ltd
London   New York   Toronto

© P N Vanezis 1971
First published in the UK in 1971
First published in the USA in 1972
ISBN 0 200 71858 4
LCCC NO 74–166536

LONDON
Abelard-Schuman
Limited
8 King Street
WC2

NEW YORK
Abelard-Schuman
Limited
257 Park Avenue South
NY 10010

TORONTO
Abelard-Schuman
Canada Limited
228 Yorkland Boulevard
425

Contents

List of Illustrations

LIST OF ILLUSTRATIONS

Acknowledgements

The author would like to acknowledge the invaluable assistance he has derived in preparing this work from the sources he has quoted in the text and would like to mention in particular the cited works of Mr. Robert Stephens, General George Grivas and Captain Le Geyt.

For the general background to the Cyprus problem and the E.O.K.A. struggle, the guidance and help derived from the distinguished Cypriot author, Doros Alastos, and the veteran journalist, Charles Foley (editor of *The Times of Cyprus* and editor of the Grivas diaries), must be especially mentioned.

Thanks are also due to Mr. L. Haber for his help in the preparation of the manuscript.

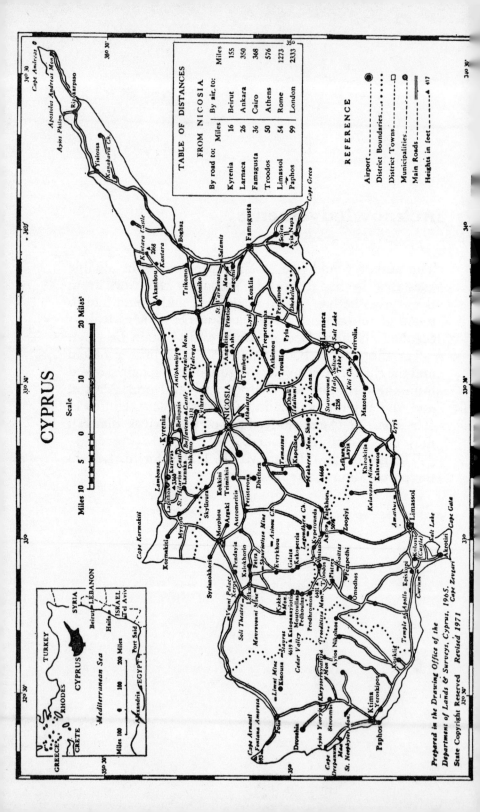

CYPRUS

Scale

Miles 10   5   0   5   10   15   20 Miles

TABLE OF DISTANCES

FROM NICOSIA

By road to:	Miles		By air to:	Miles
Kyrenia	16		Beirut	155
Larnaca	26		Ankara	350
Famagusta	36		Cairo	368
Troodos	50		Athens	576
Limassol	54		Rome	1273
Paphos	99		London	2133

REFERENCE

Airport	⦿
District Boundaries	• • • • •
District Towns	☐
Municipalities	⊚
Main Roads	——
Heights in feet	▲ 417

Prepared in the Drawing Office of the
Department of Lands & Surveys, Cyprus, 1965, Revised 1971
State Copyright Reserved

Introduction

Only the other day, just before returning to my home in London, I was sitting with Archbishop Makarios in the garden of the Presidential Palace in the somewhat distracting and unreal circumstances of making a film. There is to me a certain extra dimension of fantasy in this place, which I had known well for a number of tense and depressing years as the residence of colonial governors, and which still wears a huge masonry British coat of arms above the main door. 'Why not?' asks Makarios, whenever the anomaly is questioned. 'We preserve the relics of all the past occupations—Roman ruins, Venetian fortifications. This will be a candidate for an antiquity one day.'

These television interviews presuppose certain rites and formulae expected both from the intruder and the subject, and we dutifully disposed of the customary banalities. That done, it occurred to me to say impulsively that the curious bonds that have always seemed to exist between the Hellenic and British societies had somehow visibly survived some very terrible vicissitudes, including the dismal episode of the 1950's. Did he, I wondered, as a pragmatist, believe that this intuitive background sympathy was in fact a humbug or a reality? Archbishop Makarios allowed his cryptic expression to break into that sudden momentary smile that disarms almost everyone and said: 'I do believe that in spite of everything that it has an inexplicable reality.'

This is what I also believe. Whatever it is, it survived the emergency, it survived Anthony Eden, it survived Grivas, it survived Harding, it will survive the colonels of Athens. In a world of international expediency and political double-think the intuitive affinity between Greeks and British is an enduring and indeed inexplicable imponderable.

*   *   *

It is always hard to recall exactly when an old love-affair began—or indeed sometimes even why. My own commitment to Cyprus originated in the summer of 1954, the year of the great negatives: that is, when Eden told Marshal Papagos in Athens that there wasn't nor could ever be a Cyprus problem to be discussed with the Greek government; and when Henry Hopkinson, Colonial Minister of State, told Parliament that there were 'certain territories in the Commonwealth which can never expect to be fully independent'. However inadvertent and petulant these categorical 'no's were, they urged me down to Cyprus (which I had known before but casually) to see this place apparently consigned to political limbo for eternity.

I arrived more or less as the Cyprus Attorney General announced that any advocacy in favour of *enosis*, written or spoken, would constitute sedition and be punishable by imprisonment up to five years and, in the case of newspapers, suspension up to three years. This struck me, as a liberal journalist for a liberal newspaper, as a truly extraordinary state of affairs: that the one paramount issue of popular debate in a technical democracy should actually be outlawed from public discussion. This seemed to me to presage, without the slightest doubt, the troubles that did in fact ensue.

Since even the *argument* of *enosis* was made illegal, I hastened to write a full-page article for my paper, the late *News Chronicle*, in which I propounded the forbidden argument as fully as I could, and for good measure printed the word *enosis* in Greek eight times as a crosshead all over the page, which I hoped might simultaneously inform the authorities and provoke them. This, of course, it did, and the legal department so put the wind up the Nicosia newsagents that my newspaper went deeper under the counter than the *Kama Sutra* and was changing hands at five bob a copy. My own position remained invidious and obscure while the legal department brooded on how far the anti-sedition Ordinance applied to a visiting and articulate writer with an evident chip on his shoulder. That it was somebody else's chip made it all the more complicated.

The point was—and for that matter still is—that I held no personal brief for *enosis* or for anything else that was a wholly Cypriot concern. At the time I held it, as a political proposition, to be the most strangely emotional yearning, the most admirably senseless yet certain romanticism: ineradicable. The arguments that I made then I would not make now—and nor, indeed, would President Makarios. But in those days the nature of the argument was of less importance to me than that the argument should be made, despite the paradoxes, despite the dilemmas, despite the fears. All this is long ago, in what we may call the Pre-Zürich Period or Early-Naafi Age; it seems far away now, in the light of what has happened, but it explains my small involvement, and my right to introduce this work, because thus I made many friends in Cyprus. They were not all like-minded, which was their value to me. They, too, endure.

It was at this time that I first met Archbishop Makarios. I called on him at the old Archbishopric—a strange rickety place of a certain archaic charm that is rather missed, to my taste, by its elegant successor. His alienation from the colonial administration was a great surprise to me; it was clear that H.M.G. had done very little homework on the unique relationship between the Ethnarch of his Church and his community, in a social and political sense; I know they thought of him—at least to begin with—simply as a turbulent priest. I learned more as time went on; I am unsure whether H.M.G. ever did. However, at the time I saw quite a lot of the Archbishop. My awe was marginally modified when I learned that despite the patriarchal beard and the canonicals he was a year or two younger than I; this I found encouraging. In many years to come we were to discover a common experience of being, for different reasons, stuck in the Seychelles. Of such trifles are associations born.

I am not committing here the impertinence of recommending Dr. Vanezis' book on Makarios. Dr. Vanezis knows more about Makarios, about Cyprus, about the whole complex of love-hate values that have so long informed our relationship than I shall ever know. Dr. Vanezis is a man of Cyprus, with his roots in Britain. I am a man of Britain—I suppose—with the diffident confidence of hoping I have at least one or two tentative capillary roots in Cyprus. In our short time we have, God knows, seen the thesis and the antithesis of a multitude of misunderstandings: the synthesis is there and I know we shall find it.

James Cameron

Preface

The idea of a modern state of which the head is the prelate of the Church is very uncomfortable in our times. The whole history of Western Europe has been one of increasing separation between Church and State. Churchmen have been steadily eliminated from holding offices under the State, let alone from being heads of State.[1] This tendency has been greatly accelerated by the French Revolution, which proclaimed the secular nature of the State and wiped out traces of feudalism throughout Europe. It comes as a shock, therefore, that in the second half of the 20th century an Archbishop should be the President of a Republic which also happens to be a member of the British Commonwealth. If, in addition, the most unhappy history of Cyprus and the present crisis threatening to engulf that island are taken into consideration, then the bewilderment and confusion in this matter becomes more apparent. It is also necessary to add that Archbishop Makarios III is a bishop of the Greek Orthodox Church and as such attracts a lot of prejudice—the residue of ancient theological hatreds between East and West which very possibly affect, subconsciously, people who regard themselves as Protestants or profess indifference to religious rivalries. The cry goes up too easily: 'Byzantine!' and 'Hypocrite!'.

For a truly unprejudiced person, different standards

apply to different situations in different parts of the world. It can come as a shock to some western European people to realize that eastern Europe and Russia have not been on the whole affected by the course of western European history. As far as the southern part of this area is concerned, namely the Balkans and what is called the Near East, it must be realized that these lands, once the cradle of ancient civilization, have for centuries formed part of the Ottoman Empire and that Ottoman power in the eastern Mediterranean had once been one of the permanent features of that area. Nor is it realized that the Ottoman Empire, although once upon a time an extremely powerful state, was also one of the most conservative conceptions that the world has ever seen. It was precisely Ottoman rule that had kept its subjects —both Turkish and non-Turkish—in medieval conditions. For various reasons Ottoman rule could only flourish if the subjects of the Ottomans retained a medieval structure of society. In addition, in confrontation with its Christian subjects, an element of religious hostility was brought in. No wonder that churchmen continued to be the leaders of Christian communities in the Ottoman Empire and as such both expressed and earned hostility of the Moslems. When nationalism struck the Ottoman Empire, beginning with the Greek War of Independence, it was only natural that prelates and priests should become the leaders of the subjugated Christian communities in their struggle for freedom. In other parts of the world where nationalism also manifested itself there was no lack of other leaders: landowners, capitalists, military leaders and other middle-class elements. But in the Ottoman Empire, where the growth of a middle class had been restricted, the subject Christian population did not possess any other leaders except its bishops and priests, and this had always been the intention of the Ottoman authorities. Therefore, as nationalist struggles bit into the decaying carcass of the Ottoman Empire, ecclesiastics of the Orthodox Church were always well in the lead. They had been made the national leaders of their communities while their profession made them implacable opponents of the Moslem Turks. Orthodox bishops and priests in the Near East were freed by the tide of nationalism to become politicians and even soldiers. The idea that a bishop should be the head of a Greek Orthodox State carved out of the body of the Ottoman Empire is not anachronistic but perfectly normal, as there were hardly any other candidates for this office.

Cyprus provides an even better example of this process. Historically the Church of Cyprus is distinguished and greatly privileged. The Archbishops of Cyprus were recognized as spokesmen for their island by Byzantine emperors, Turkish sultans and their British successors after 1878. This was not only a convenient arrangement, but it was legalized and formalized under the Ottoman Empire in the 17th Century, by the *berat*, a decree from the Sultan conferring on the Archbishops of Cyprus powers as administrative, judicial and political heads of their community. Henceforth no administration of Cyprus would have been carried out without their co-operation. This state of affairs was recognized by the British government when Cyprus was occupied in 1878, as legally the island remained a part of the Ottoman Empire until 1915. In 1923 after the First World War the Ottoman regime in Cyprus was extinguished by the Treaty of Lausanne, but despite this the Archbishops of Cyprus remained in reality the recognized leaders of their community. The picture is completed by the fact that the Archbishops of Cyprus are elected by a democratic electoral process which includes the whole male population of the island, thus providing the necessary democratic element without which no successful nationalist leaders can function.

Archbishop Makarios became the Archbishop of Cyprus not in the age of classical nationalism but in the age of anti-colonialism. He was the ideal leader of the anti-colonialist struggle of Cyprus: the only anti-colonialist leader in the British Empire not trained at Oxford or Cambridge, the Bar or one of the London teaching hospitals. This fact made him greatly suspect in British eyes, despite his cloth and his high principles, and has subjected him to a degree of abuse from the British press that has hardly been the lot of any other nationalist leader of different colour, creed or profession.

This book attempts to correlate the Cyprus problem to the historical evolution of the decay of the Ottoman Empire and the course of nationalism in its successor states. The very fact that Greece and Turkey became nearly involved in war over Cyprus, in which Russia would have probably intervened, manifests the fact that Cyprus is an integral part of the Near East problem. At present all is quiet on the Cyprus front, but the future is obscure. Throughout this the figure of Archbishop Makarios acquires an enigmatic posture. Makarios, is he a power-hungry politician or a self-effacing churchman? Is he a front for reaction or is he a rallying point for democrats? Will he persevere with the dangerous task of uniting Cyprus with Greece or will he prefer to be the President of a separate and independent Cyprus? It is difficult to answer all these questions as Archbishop Makarios is truly Byzantine in that he is inscrutable. This book attempts to shed some light on the man, his country, and the problems they represent.

PART A

PART A

I
Cyprus: The Island

Of all the islands of the Greek world Cyprus is the largest (3,572 square miles), although the most distant from the Greek mainland; geographically the island is part of Asia, being only 60 miles from Syria and 40 miles from Turkey. In such circumstances it should really have been part of the Eastern world if not for the accidents of history.

From the physical point of view there is little difference between Cyprus and the other islands of the Aegean, both the Cyclades and the Dodecanese, as it is mountainous, a typical feature of that region. There are two mountain ranges in Cyprus stretching from east to west, one in the north-east and the other, the major, the Troodos range in the south-west. Between these two ranges the centre of the island is occupied by the chief agricultural plain, the Mesaoria, where the main centre of population, the capital Nicosia, is situated. Around the coast at the foot of the mountain ranges are situated the famous harbours of Cyprus, Famagusta in the east, Larnaca, Limassol and Ktima (Paphos) in the south, and Morphou and Kyrenia in the north.

The soil and climate of Cyprus are of the typical Mediterranean variety—mild winters with moderate rainfalls and hot, arid summers. This is responsible for the fact that agriculture in Cyprus is of the typical

Mediterranean variety. The soil is very fertile and owing to limited water supply needs constant irrigation and application of hydraulic techniques. In this situation the economy is based more on the control of water than on the ownership of land. Water rights are bought and sold and have always regulated the cycle of agriculture. This has always been the traditional practice in Mediterranean countries, which very few people brought up in the more humid countries to the north appreciate.

According to the latest census, 50 per cent of the total area of the island is under cultivation. The principal crops are cereals, legumes and potatoes, and such vegetables as carrots, tomatoes and cucumbers. Since antiquity Cyprus has been also celebrated for its fruit and wine. The island produces all deciduous fruits such as apples, pears, plums, peaches, apricots and cherries.

The olive tree is cultivated everywhere, particularly in the sea-facing slopes of the two ranges, and, as elsewhere in the Mediterranean, it is the principal source of fat for human consumption. Wine in Cyprus has been mentioned in Homer who commented on its deep, dark colour, and has been cultivated continuously both for home consumption and export. Cyprus wines together with other Mediterranean wines from Crete, Sicily and Spain were well known and consumed, particularly in England, long before the more recent ascendancy of the lighter French wines. However, the French Lusignan rule in Cyprus during the Middle Ages resulted in the production of French-type wines as early as that period and the growth of the wine-making industry in recent years has resulted in the production of certain excellent light table wines, both red and white, for the European market. In addition Cyprus grapes and raisins are highly regarded abroad due to the qualities imparted to them by the soil and climate of Cyprus which seems to be the native land of viticulture. Indeed, as early as biblical times we read in the Song of Solomon, Chapter I: 'My beloved is unto me as a cluster of Cyprus grapes...' Other agricultural produce are potatoes, melons, figs and tobacco. In recent years citrus cultivation has made rapid strides in Cyprus and the island is now one of the chief exporters of oranges, grapefruit and lemons in the Middle East.

Cyprus is also the world's chief producer of carobs or locust beans, which are one of the island's principal exports. The carob tree is as typical of Cyprus as the mulberry tree is typical of the Peloponnese. The popularity of the carobs in various Mediterranean countries, both for human and animal consumption, is associated with legends concerning St. John the Baptist, based on the misunderstanding that he ate carobs (locust beans) instead of the actual locust in the desert and hence in many countries the carob pod with its beans is known as St. John's bread.

The arid and mountainous nature of Cyprus, like most of the Mediterranean countries, does not make the island a dairy-farming area. Most domestic animals are sheep and goats reared for their flesh and wool and which graze in the arid parts of the plains or on the bare mountains. In the Troodos mountains a species of large-horned wild sheep, the mouflon, is found. This animal is native to Cyprus and survives because of government protection. There are no other large animals in Cyprus except for some wolves in the northern Kyrenia range.

Under the soil of Cyprus have been found since ancient times such minerals as copper, chromium, iron and asbestos. The presence of copper in Cyprus together with the antiquity of the copper mines has given rise to the argument that either the name of Cyprus is derived from

23

the word copper or is itself a corruption of copper. The struggle to control the copper mines of Cyprus was one of the chief features of power politics in the ancient world. Copper is still today the principal non-agricultural export of Cyprus.

The capital of Cyprus is Nicosia (Lefkosia—formerly Ledra in classical times) situated in a strategic position between the two mountain ranges commanding the main road to Kyrenia, the principal harbour on the northern coast facing the coast of Asia Minor. It has a population today of around 100,000. The centre of the town is circular and surrounded by walls and bastions constructed by the Lusignan rulers and their Venetian successors. This was the Nicosia assaulted by the Turks during their conquest of the island in 1571. Since that date it became their H.Q.

There has been conspicuous Turkish settlement in Nicosia which obliterated the original medieval character of the old town. The Gothic cathedral and churches of the Catholic Lusignans and Venetians were turned into mosques with minarets marring the original proportions and surrounding them with twisting and dirty narrow streets and lanes. The modern part of Nicosia, exclusively Greek in character, is today situated outside the old walls, providing a complete contrast with its wide roads, tall modern buildings, schools and hospitals.

On the east coast is situated the principal port of Cyprus, Famagusta, among sandy beaches which gave this town its original name of Ammochostos (hidden in the sand). This town replaced in Byzantine and medieval times the ancient city of Salamis, situated to the north of it, which played a very prominent part in early Cypriot history. The old town of Famagusta was surrounded by magnificent Gothic walls built by the Lusignans and Venetians and used to be, during the

Middle Ages, the centre of Italian trade in the Levant. Today, as in Nicosia, the Gothic town with its churches is mainly inhabited by the Turks while the Greek population is concentrated to the south in the modern suburb of Varoshia or New Famagusta.

On the south coast is situated the town of Larnaca, in ancient times the Phoenician colony of Kition, the birthplace of Zeno, founder of the Stoic School of Philosophy.[1] The population is about 20,000, but during the Ottoman rule in Cyprus it used to be a busy port and the H.Q. of all the foreign consuls.

Continuing along the south coast of the island where the Troodos mountains meet the sea is the town of Limassol, with a population of 45,000; it is the second town of Cyprus after Nicosia, and the principal industrial town of the island. Its economic importance has been enhanced in recent days by its proximity to the chief British military base in Cyprus situated on the Akrotiri peninsula. Its port is today, perhaps, the busiest in the island and the chief outlet for the wine trade.

On the western coast of the island, about a mile from the shore, is situated the town of Ktima. Ktima has replaced in modern times the celebrated city of Paphos on the coast .The whole area is full of ancient monuments as it was the original centre of Hellenic settlement in Cyprus in pre-classical times, the centre of the cult of Aphrodite and the preserved birthplace of that goddess, also the capital of Cyprus in Roman times.

The principal towns on the north coast of Cyprus are Morphou and Kyrenia. The first, lying due west of Nicosia on Morphou Bay, is situated inland in the middle of a rich alluvial plain, well watered, and is the centre of the island's growing citrus fruit industry. Kyrenia is situated due north of Nicosia across the Pentadaktylos mountain range. It is the most romantic town in Cyprus, dominated by its medieval castles and fortifications. Near it are such gems of medieval Cyprus Gothic architecture as the castles of St. Hilarion and Buffavento and the celebrated Abbey of Bellapais. The harbour of Kyrenia is considered to be the most beautiful in Cyprus and a great favourite of the English ex-service personnel.

Practically the whole of the south and the south-west of Cyprus is dominated by the Troodos massif. Here is the Heart of Cyprus. In the east, upland valleys are forests and dedicated to the Holy Virgin. In winter the mountain valleys are covered by snow and skiing has become a popular sport. Needless to say, this mountain region was the stronghold of the E.O.K.A. guerrilla forces during their four-year struggle against the British rule of the island.

II
Cyprus: The People

In recent times a great deal of ingenuity has been exerted in certain quarters in order to prove that the Greek population of the island of Cyprus is not Greek. For this purpose they were called 'Greek-speaking', 'Greek-Christian' or simply 'Orthodox' and 'Greek Orthodox'. This solicitude to create a new type of population in Cyprus would have puzzled and amused the old Ottoman rulers of Cyprus and the rest of the Greek world. For them a Greek was a Greek—and unmistakably at that, whether he was living in Cyprus, Constantinople, Athens, Crete or Alexandria. The simple criterion of language and religion was enough to establish this fact without the demotic appeal to racialism and manipulated cultural history. It must not be forgotten that at the time of the Greek War of Independence (1821–30) an ingenious Austrian, Professor Fallmerayer, came out with his celebrated thesis that the Greeks were not Greeks but Slavs and Albanians. This astonishing discovery was meant to be of great importance, as if it mattered what blood people have in their veins and what their physical appearance is when they all speak a certain language and profess a certain religion. The fact that the Jews of the Diaspora look very unlike each other and speak different languages is nevertheless subordinated to the central fact that having a common religion they have a common mentality, feel themselves to be Jews, and would never be failed to be recognized as Jews by anyone else. What was battling against the Turks in Greece while Fallmerayer was expounding his thesis was not Greek blood and classical physiques but the Greek language and the Greek Orthodox Christian religion which gave the people of Greece, whatever their actual physical origin, a common heritage and a sense of community, i.e. because they spoke Greek and held the Greek belief they could think of themselves as nothing but Greek, even if they had Slav ancestors.

It is unfortunate that in recent years the most clumsy racialist arguments have been used by Turkish press and propaganda with regard to Cyprus, and have found their sycophants in Britain, in such different quarters as the Colonial Office and the popular press. These arguments reiterate the fact that in very early times Cyprus and the rest of Asia Minor were occupied by non-Aryan tribes which were, therefore, Turkish or Mongoloid and so related to the modern Turks. Another argument, more ingenious, pleads that the original population of Cyprus was of Hittite origin and, as the Hittites formed part of the population of Asia Minor, they were absorbed by the conquering Turks who thus have the same blood in their veins as the people of Cyprus. The arguments are untenable for two reasons: one, even if the people of Cyprus are not Greek by blood they are not Turkish because they are Greek by language and culture; two, the historical arguments advanced to prove the non-Hellenic blood of the Greek Cypriots are false. The Greeks of Cyprus are predominantly Greek in blood as well as being Greek in language and culture. Sir Ronald Storrs, Governor of the island for six years writes: 'The Greekness of Cypriots is, in my opinion, indisputable. Nationalism, is more, is other, is greater than pigmentations or cephalic indices. A man is of the race of which he passionately feels himself to be. No sensible person will deny that the Cypriot is Greek-speaking, Greek-thinking, Greek-feeling, Greek, just as much as the French Canadian is French-speaking, French-thinking, French-feeling and French.'[1]

In very early times Cyprus, Asia Minor and Syria were inhabited by much the same kind of people, though who and what they were is difficult to tell. Consequently Cyprus came under the influence of ancient Egypt and the Cretan and Mycenean civilizations. Crete and the Mycenean civilization of the Aegean were in the West, and there the first link was established between Cyprus and the Western world, and nobody can deny that Cretan and Mycenean cultures formed the basis of classical Greek civilization. There is evidence that settlement of western Cyprus began around the first millennium B.C. when the Achaean Greeks driven out by the Darians appeared in Cyprus where they proceeded to establish typical Greek city states. At the same time a Semitic Phoenician movement began into eastern Cyprus, and Chittins (as mentioned in the Bible) called by the Greeks Kition became the Chief Phoenician state in Cyprus. In 709 B.C., when Cyprus was under the rule of Assyria, the King of Assyria inscribed on a monument found at Larnaca the names of the kings of the cities of Cyprus who did him homage. Some of these names are Greek, others are Phoenician or native. By native would be meant either the pre-Hellenic and pre-Phoenician population of Cyprus or the Minoan-Mycenean element. Thereafter Greek influence in Cyprus takes on the form of a predominant culture. Greek mythology chose Cyprus to be the birthplace of Aphrodite and her temple at Paphos gave Cyprus an unsurpassed religious significance in the Hellenic world.

The office of the High Priest of the Temple of Aphrodite at Paphos became of such importance that it was offered by the Romans to one of the royal family of the Ptolemies as compensation for a lost kingdom. Homer regarded Cyprus to be in Greek land and, after Homer, the rest of the Greek tragedians did likewise. In Cyprus itself Greek literature flourished and Cyprus produced the Greek epic poet Stassinos who celebrated his native island in a poem called 'Cypria' in the 7th century B.C.

Although Cyprus came to be dominated by Egypt, Assyria and Persia, its Greek character asserted itself and deepened. The principal Greek kingdoms in Cyprus were Salamis, Curium, Paphos, Marion, Soli, Kyrenia and Chytri. Particularly during the period of Persian domination the great king of Salamis, Evagoras, asserted Greek and Athenian influence in Cyprus and, although native elements still lurked beneath the surface, Cyprus was henceforth regarded by the Athenians as being fully within the ambit of Greek civilization.

The basic event which, however, attached Cyprus finally to the Hellenic world occurred when the Greeks of Cyprus joined Alexander the Great in his war against the Persians and the Phoenicians. From that day on Cyprus became entirely Greek and the Phoenician cities were absorbed and turned into Greek states. The Phoenician population was absorbed very quickly by the dominant Hellenic element.

After the break-up of Alexander's Empire Cyprus became attached to the Eygptian kingdom of the Ptolemies and from the hands of the Ptolemies it passed into the hands of Rome. The next most important factor in Cypriot history was the division of the Roman Empire between East and West. Cyprus was within the Eastern Empire of Byzantium which in time—and particularly after the loss of Asiatic and African territories to the Moslems—became a Greek national state, Greek in language, Greek in religion and Greek in feeling. Cyprus was a province, and at times a very important province of Byzantium until in 1196 it became detached from the Empire by the treason of the tyrant Isaac Comnenos and from his hands it was snatched by the Crusaders, to remain under foreign rule—Crusader, Lusignan, Venetian, Turkish and British—until 1959. Thus Cyprus, detached by foreigners from its Byzantine Greek motherland, lived on under alien masters while the Byzantine Empire itself fell and disappeared and Greece rose again in the 19th century.

From the 13th to the 16th century Cyprus was under the rule of Westerners. Until the 15th century Cyprus was a sovereign kingdom under the House of Lusignan, with its own kings, who acquired in addition the shadowy towns of Jerusalem and Armenia. In the 15th century it became simply a Venetian colony up to the time of its conquest by the Ottoman rulers in 1570-1. During the Lusignan period the France-dominated kingdom of Cyprus was one of the jewels of western European medieval civilization, transplanted to the Eastern Mediterranean. It was the only crusader state in the East which made good; its survival and success were due to its insular position. As such it became the principal base for Western commercial enterprise in the Levant, and, as well as the crusading French feudal establishment, numerous Western merchants, etc.—mainly from the commercial cities of Italy—settled in its cities. However, the absolute bar of religion prevented any significant mingling between the Western merchants and the native Greek population.

The end of the Lusignan kingdom in the 15th century combined with Venetian rule and, therefore, Venetian

31

trade monopoly and the rise of Ottoman power, caused the disappearance of the medieval crusading element from Cyprus. By the time of the Ottoman attack the only Western elements in Cyprus were the Venetian garrison and merchants and the Latin clergy. As elsewhere in the Levant, the Crusaders left behind them in Cyprus only memories and ruins without having impressed their stamp on the population.

The Ottoman conquest was very different, and the nature of its difference has been responsible for the subsequent development of Cyprus and its destiny, as has been the case wherever the House of Ottoman held sway. The Seljuk and Ottoman Turks, nomadic tribes in origin, were not so much an army as a people on the march. Like true nomads they settled down where they conquered if they liked the land or found it strategically necessary to do so. Furthermore, it has always been a standard Ottoman practice (partly from necessity and partly in imitation of the Romans) to pay their troops with land grants and to settle colonies of Moslem soldiers amid alien and hostile, i.e. Christian, populations. Thus it came about that the Ottoman garrison in Cyprus settled down with their families and became in time a permanent part of the population of the island, cultivating the soil side by side with the Greek islanders. However, once again the bar of religion kept the two communities apart and, although in time most of the Turks in Cyprus gained some knowledge of Greek, the two communities have remained separate in religion, language and feeling till the present day. With good foundation, Charles Foley states in his book *Legacy of Strife*: '. . . Cyprus is, after all, a Greek island and has remained so through many centuries and many foreign occupations. The Turks were merely the last interlopers there before the British came. For years they were used, in time of need, as a stick to beat the Greeks; when left alone, they overplayed their hand.'

The Turks are, and always have been, a population *in* Cyprus but not *of* Cyprus, and only the passing of Cyprus under British rule in 1878 shelved this matter of a Turkish garrison in a Greek island which had formed part of the Ottoman Empire, or of a Turkish minority in a Greek Cyprus either independent or united with Greece. The military nature of the Turkish settlement in Cyprus has also been responsible for the fact that Turkish communities (up to 1964) had been dispersed throughout the island without being concentrated in any one particular part of it except in the case of the old parts of Nicosia and Famagusta.[2]

It is interesting to note that after 1878, under British rule, the Turkish minority in Cyprus,[3] because of the separation from Turkey, was the only Turkish community which did not undergo the experience of the Tanzimat period under Midhat Pasha, the Young Turk Revolution, the experience of Turkey in the First World War, followed by the Kemalist revolution and the subsequent Kemalist regime in Turkey. Accordingly, except for Greek and British influence, the Cypriot Turks belong more in feeling to the old traditional Turkey rather than the Turkish Republic of today. At least their fear and mistrust of the Greeks is reminiscent of the religious and national hatreds of the 19th century, and has helped to keep alive in the eastern Mediterranean the traditional Balkan atmosphere wrought with so many dangers and apprehensions.

As far as the Greek population of Cyprus is concerned, the British occupation of the island in 1878 was a liberation of still one more Greek community from Ottoman domination and a logical step on the road towards union with an independent Greece which had arisen in the

c

first half of the 19th century and the only political principle of which would be the liberation of all the remaining Greek soil from foreign, i.e. Ottoman, rule. The end of Ottoman rule in Cyprus meant that cultural and political contacts between Athens and the Greek population of Cyprus increased and became more intimate, and this was achieved very often with British co-operation and goodwill. This tendency became even more accentuated after 1914 when Turkey found itself at war with Britain and Britain formally proclaimed Cyprus to be a crown colony no longer connected in any way with the Ottoman Empire. Greece, on the other hand, became an ally of Britain in 1916, and great hopes were raised that an allied victory over Turkey would bring about the liberation of all Greek communities under Turkish rule and the union of all Greek territories with a greater and stronger Greece. The complications which prevented the implementation of this desire were responsible for the growth of bitterness among the Greeks of Cyprus, which culminated in the events of 1931. After 1931 the development of the situation was such that hostility of the Greeks of Cyprus towards Britain had to come to a head and it was only the crisis leading to the Second World War and the cause of that war itself which masked this situation and delayed a violent outburst.

The conclusion must be that the Greek character of the population of Cyprus has never been denied until the present day though it is true that, in common with other Greek islands, the Greeks of Cyprus are different in some details from the continental Greeks, particularly the Athenians, but this is no new phenomenon and can be encountered in many other countries. It is also true that Cyprus has been continuously under foreign rule from 1191 to 1959, but except for the Turkish garrison which arrived in 1571, and settled down on the land, all the other foreign rulers of the island remained as such and departed when their time was done. That they left such material evidence of their presence as buildings, etc., does not prove that they had in any way succeeded in altering the people. It must also be remembered that Greece itself had been ruled by Romans, Crusaders and Turks for many centuries but the Greeks remained Greeks. It is foolish to argue, because of vested interests, that Cyprus is a special case and that what applies to Cyprus does not apply to Greece or vice versa. The best evidence, after all, is supplied by both the Turkish element in Cyprus and the Government of Turkey who hardly ever refer to the people of Cyprus as Cypriots, but always as Greeks.

III
Cyprus and the Orthodox Church

The position of Archbishop Makarios both in the political struggles prior to 1959 and afterwards as the President of Cyprus is due entirely to the fact that Cyprus is a Greek Orthodox land reflecting time-honoured Byzantine traditions. The preponderance of bishops in the Byzantine political system has an ancient ascendancy. The European Justinian associated bishops with the civil governors and transferred political powers to them in the absence of civil authorities. Thus, for instance, when the city of Rome became cut off by Lombard conquest from the seat of the Byzantine governor (exarch) at Ravenna, the Bishop of Rome became the political head of his territory. This, and not the legendary Donation of Constantine, has been responsible for the political and territorial power of the papacy by making the Pope a territorial prince. The whole period of Turkish and foreign domination of the Greeks has been a period which marked the disappearance of civil authority, hence the political power and role of the Greek bishops. It must not be forgotten that in 1821 Archbishop Germanos led the original revolt of the Greeks against the Turks in the Peloponnese and it was only the intervention of the major European powers in the struggle which was responsible for the fact that independent Greece was established ultimately as a kingdom and did not emerge as a state ruled by an archbishop. However, in neighbouring Montenegro the bishop was also the territorial prince and only transformed himself into a king in the second half of the 19th century. Even in recent Greek history at the end of the Second World War the Primate of Greece, Archbishop Damaskenos of Athens, acted as regent and head of the government. It seems, therefore, that because of its persistence the Orthodox Church and its bishops continue to be lieutenants, in the spirit of Justinian, of the vanished emperor at Constantinople, and continue to exercise his authority over the Orthodox until such day as the Greek-Byzantine state is restored. Therefore, foreign as the concept may be to western European thought, there is nothing unprecedented or original in the career of Archbishop Makarios, except for his youth at its outset and his persistence and political astuteness throughout.

The ignorance in western European countries of the history and tradition of the Orthodox Church is such that a brief restatement of its history is never amiss. The Orthodox Church is really a group of churches derived from the first churches founded in the East by the apostles, and particularly by the apostle Paul. They are united in dogma but are not subordinate to each other being, as they describe themselves, autocephalous. At the time of the Byzantine Empire the Orthodox churches within its territory were subject to the Emperor and supervised by the Patriarch of Constantinople. But even in Byzantine times, autocephalic churches of the Orthodox creed came into being for historical reasons in Bulgaria, Serbia, Georgia and Russia. After the destruction of the Byzantine Empire, the Patriarch of Constantinople acquired two functions, one internal and one external. The internal function with which he was endowed by the

Turkish conquerors was to be the representative and
spokesman of all the Orthodox subjects of the Sultan.
The external function, as far as Orthodox churches
outside the Ottoman Empire were concerned, was to
act as an honorary president of the Orthodox faith
(Ecumenical Patriarch). The Patriarch of Constantinople, unlike the Pope in the West, has never been
anything like the absolute head of a united and central-
ized Church, which ignored frontiers and nationalities.

It is not often realized that the Orthodox Church of
Cyprus is one of the oldest Christian churches of the
world, much older than the Patriarchate of Constantinople itself or the Church of metropolitan Greece. The
Church of Cyprus was one of the original churches
founded by St. Paul who together with St. John visited
Cyprus, preached Christianity there, converting the
Roman governor, Sergius Paulus, and consecrated
St. Barnabas, a native of Cyprus although a Jew, to be
the first bishop of the island. Thus Cyprus is almost
unique in having had one of its natives as its first consecrated bishop, a fact which confers a great amount of
prestige on the Church of Cyprus, and, throughout its
history up to the present day, only natives of Cyprus have
sat on the throne of St. Barnabas. This distinction
enjoyed by the Church of Cyprus became of great
importance when the Roman Empire became Christian.
The Bishops of Cyprus always claimed independence
from the Patriarchs of Antioch, who maintained that
Cyprus was a part of their province. The Church of
Cyprus, however, was the first Christian church to
advance a claim to autocephality, because of its apostolic
foundation, at the Council of Ephesus in A.D. 413.
Actually, the autocephality of the Church of Cyprus was
confirmed by the Emperor Zeno in 478 after the miraculous discovery by the Archbishop of Cyprus, Anthemios,

of the body of the martyred St. Barnabas buried together with a copy of St. Matthew's Gospel, which he presented to the Emperor. Thus, the Church of Cyprus became fully autocephalous, ranking in orthodoxy as fifth after Jerusalem, Antioch, Alexandria and Constantinople, and senior to the Churches of Georgia, Bulgaria, Serbia, Russia, Rumania and Greece.[1]

Also, because of the miraculous discovery mentioned above, the Emperor bestowed on the Archbishop of Cyprus the distinctive privileges of wearing the imperial purple, having the imperial sceptre instead of the usual episcopal staff and signing his name and title in imperial purple ink—privileges which the Archbishops of Cyprus have jealously preserved until this day. Such imperial dignities bestowed on the Archbishops of Cyprus accorded very well with Justinian's later disposition mentioned before, which endowed bishops with political authority. In Cyprus the Archbishop became the recognized head of the whole island, enjoying precedence over the civil authorities and responsible directly to the Emperor. It should be obvious from all this that, in the Orthodox view, the Church of Cyprus, being of direct apostolic origin, ranks equal in Christian theory with all the other churches established by the apostles, including that of Rome, and the Archbishops of Cyprus are the equals of the Apostolic Patriarchs of Jerusalem, Antioch, Alexandria, Constantinople, and the Pope in Rome. As the apostolic origins of the Church of Constantinople are somewhat doubtful, it may well be that the Church of Cyprus is the senior apostolic church in the Greek world as it is today. Accordingly, it seems inconceivable, given the prestige and venerability of the Church of Cyprus, that it should have been treated with such lack of respect as events have shown.

History seems to have imposed on Cyprus the role of

a front-line battlefield. In the 7th century the rapid Arab conquest of the Middle East made Cyprus the most exposed province of the Eastern Empire. For 300 years, each time the Caliphate was under a strong ruler and disposed of strong naval forces, Cyprus was invaded and devastated. The position of the Archbishop in these years became that of the Commander-in-Chief. Cyprus was only made safe from the Moslems in the 10th century by the victories over the Moslems of the Emperors Niciphoros Phokas and John Tsimiskis. For the next two centuries the peace of Cyprus was not disturbed. This was a period of peaceful development during which the great monasteries of Cyprus, Kykko, Macheras and Enklistra flourished. In the Orthodox world, particularly after the destruction of the monasteries of Asia Minor and Constantinople, the monasteries of Cyprus rank second only to Mount Athos and the St. Katherine's monastery in Sinai, attracting pilgrims especially from Russia.

During these centuries the Church of Cyprus, after the loss of the oriental provinces of the Byzantine Empire, was the only autocephalous church left within the Empire, which enhanced the position of the Archbishop, making him second in rank to the Patriarch of Constantinople. However, the long agony of the Eastern Empire was approaching. Islam returned to the attack under the leadership of the Turks. In the 11th century the Seljuk Turks sealed the fate of Byzantium: they overthrew Byzantine military power in Anatolia and thereby provoked the crusading movement in western Europe. However, because of the schism between eastern and western Churches the Crusaders turned out to be even worse enemies of the Byzantine Empire than the Turks. The crusader states (Kingdom of Jerusalem, the Kingdom of the Principality of Antioch, etc.) were the enemies of both the Moslems and the Byzantines, and it did not take long for Cyprus to be raided (1155) from the crusader-dominated Syrian coast. The second and third Crusades which followed, although unsuccessful in their objective, that is the defeat of the Moslems and the recapture of Jerusalem, became expeditions aimed at the conquest of the Byzantine Empire. Richard I of England proved, in 1191, how easy it was to invade and conquer a Greek Orthodox country by his seizure of Cyprus, when Cyprus was the first Orthodox land to fall to the Latins. The conquest of the rest of the Byzantine Empire followed soon after, though there was not much left of it by that time, but this conquest, especially of Constantinople, Salonika and Athos, was much more lucrative than fighting the Seljuks. The days of the Byzantine Empire were over, though it was later to linger in the besieged city of Constantinople till 1453. The dark night of the Orthodox Church in the Greek lands had begun—and western Christians and Moslem Turks vied with each other in trampling on it.

The disappearance of the Byzantine Empire after a period of 1,000 years had many far-reaching consequences. The most obvious consequence was the invasion of the Balkans by the Turks. The other one was the subjugation of the Greek Orthodox Church among the Greeks by foreigners and infidels. Moscow alone remained as the independent Orthodox country but Moscow was not Greek.

Cyprus had the distinction of being the first Greek land to be conquered by the Latin crusaders and the last to be conquered by the Turks. The Orthodox Church of Cyprus was the first Orthodox church to be subjugated by western Christianity. The arrival and persistence for 400 years of an alien religion and an alien social and legal system drew a sharp line of distinction between the Cypriots and their new masters. The assaulted and persecuted Orthodox Church became their rallying point in their resistance to the foreigners. Throughout the Lusignan period the position of the Orthodox Church in Cyprus varied according to the personality of the Kings of Cyprus, the policy of the Popes and the crusading states in the Levant. On the whole, the Greek clergy were subordinated to the imported Latin clergy, the Archbishopric was suppressed and the Orthodox bishops expelled from the towns. Yet there is ample evidence that the Greek population, although deprived of the Archbishops, continued to rally round the Church. Indeed, their foreign masters were, in a way, obliging them to do so by having introduced into Cyprus the feudal system of land tenure. Very many Cypriot peasants were reduced to serfdom and only in the Orthodox Church could they find relief from it. One way to escape feudal impositions was for people to enroll themselves as monks and members of minor orders in various churches and monasteries, and this became so successful that the Latin clergy and nobility launched the Decree of Limassol in 1220 against this practice. But this did not break the popularity of the Orthodox Church with the people.

For instance, after the recovery of independence by a part of the Byzantine Empire at Nicaea, the expelled Orthodox Archbishop, Germanos, went there and, counselled by the Patriarch, advised the Church of Cyprus to resist the Roman tyranny despite any persecution that was to follow. There followed trials, torture and death for many Orthodox monks and priests, which confirmed the people of Cyprus in their opposition to the Lusignan order and provided their Church with martyrs.

In 1260 the Pope regulated the position of the Orthodox Church of Cyprus by the Bulla Cypria which, while it subordinated the Orthodox Church of Cyprus to Rome, allowed the Archbishop, Germanos, to return to exercise his office for life after which the Orthodox Archbishopric was abolished.

The Lusignan Kingdom in Cyprus came to an end in 1489, and Cyprus became a colony of Venice. In the meantime the last remnants of the Byzantine Empire including Constantinople had been conquered by the Ottoman Turks. Cyprus was the only Hellenic Orthodox land not under Ottoman rule, though still under alien Venetian rule. In 1571 Cyprus was finally conquered by the Ottomans, who now had under their direct rule all Hellenic Orthodox people and churches; only Rumania and Russia alone were outside the scope of Ottoman power. Territorially, the Ottoman Empire was the re-creation of the old Byzantine Empire, at its greatest extent, and the Turks extended to Cyprus the same religious toleration with which they favoured Orthodox Churches everywhere. For instance, after the Turkish conquest of 1453 the Patriarch of Constantinople was recognized as the head of all the Orthodox Christians, whether Greek or not, in the Ottoman Empire and the Bulgarian Church was subordinated to him as it had been in the days of Byzantine power. Everywhere the essentially military Turks tried to rule and administer their Christian subjects and their territories through the Christian clergy. In this they were greatly influenced and aided by the traditions of the Byzantine Orthodox Church which had been directed to such purposes before. In Cyprus, the Roman Catholic Church was suppressed and expelled with the Venetians and the only Christian Church recognized there came to be the native Orthodox Church. The Orthodox Archbishopric was revived after 300 years, and the Archbishop was officially recognized not only as the head of his Church but also

of the entire Greek community of Cyprus, and this was
conferred on him by a special decree of the Sultan known
as the *berat* which recognized Cyprus to be a nation
(Turkish word *millett*), thus providing the Archbishop
with the title of Ethnarch. This placed the Archbishop of
Cyprus in a very strong position for he was the only
recipient of the Sultan's *berat* in the Ottoman Empire
to have under him a closely knit Greek Orthodox
community due, no doubt, to the insular position of
Cyprus. The Orthodox prelates in the Ottoman Empire
who held the *berat* did not have such a closely knit
community at their disposal for most of the populations
of their respective provinces were Moslems and Slavs.

During the Ottoman period the Orthodox Church of
Cyprus revived, though physically it could still not
make up for the lost three centuries of development
which it suffered under Lusignan and Venetian rule.
Politically, however, the importance of the Archbishops
of Cyprus, an outlying island province, increased in
proportion to the decline of the Ottoman Empire which
began in the second half of the 17th century. As the
vitality of the Ottoman Empire decreased, the more its
outlying parts tended to become detached from the main
trunk. The chief danger here for the Porte was the power
and insubordination of the Turkish governors and
officials. It was not any revolt on the part of the subjects
of the Ottomans that destroyed the Turkish Empire but
the ambition and revolts of the Ottoman pashas and
governors. In these circumstances the government in
Constantinople became more and more dependent on
reliable Christian subjects with a corresponding increase
in the power, wealth, and influence of the Orthodox
clergy. In Cyprus the position and power of the Archbishop achieved an unprecedented peak in the 18th
century both in respect of the Sultan in Constantinople

and the inhabitants of Cyprus. For many reasons the Turkish pashas became entirely dependent on the Archbishop to be able to govern Cyprus and get their revenue from it. Sir Harry Luke says: '. . . by an astonishing reversal of fortune the Archbishop of Cyprus, whose office had been re-created by the Turks after being dormant for 300 years, seemed in the course of the 17th and 18th centuries the supreme power and authority over the island, and at one period wielded influence greater than that of the Turkish pasha himself.'[2] It must not be forgotten that such an Ottoman province as Cyprus was valued mainly by the amount of revenue it could produce for the Sultan and his subordinates. The object of government, therefore, was to squeeze as much as possible out of the population both Greek and Turkish. In this process the Archbishops of Cyprus had a clear advantage over the Turkish governors coming from outside. It was noted by 1820 that both Greeks and Turks were oppressed by the Archbishop and the Pasha, but, in the last resort, the Turkish peasant was governed by the Archbishop of Cyprus. Many travellers at this time commented on this great power of the Church in Cyprus.[3] The best account of relations existing in the island was given by the Spaniard Domingo Badia y Leyblich writing under the name of Ali Bey, and includes the following description: 'The Greeks are extremely submissive and respectful towards their bishops: saluting them they bow low, take off their cap and hold it before them upside down. They scarcely dare speak in their presence. It is true that for this community of slaves the bishops are rallying-points. It is through them that it preserves some kind of existence, so that it suits the people to give their prelates political importance, such as even the Turks allow them, judging by the deferential and respectful manner which they observe towards the

45

bishops. These, on their part, parade in their houses and follow a princely luxury; they never go out without a crowd of attendants, and to ascend a flight of stairs they must needs be carried by their servants.'[4] In reality the Turkish government in Cyprus was helpless. Sir H. Luke states: 'At the beginning of the 19th century the Archbishop was in fact ruling Cyprus through his control of its finances.'[5] He was the source of real authority both for Turks and Greeks and the Turks were beginning to regard the Archbishop with growing hostility since they were beginning to feel that in Cyprus, instead of being the conquerors, they were in fact the conquered. This made the position of Cyprus unique in the Ottoman Empire as it was in the Byzantine Empire and was eventually going to be in the British Empire. This was summed up by a British historian of Cyprus who, writing about Cyprus in 1785, said: 'Cyprus was the only province of the Turkish Empire in which the bishops thus became the virtual rulers of the people, and for a quarter of a century their position was unchallenged.'[6]

The period of the ascendancy of the Archbishops of Cyprus and the Greek dragoman dependent on them came to an end, obviously, at the time of the Greek War of Independence. Although the hierarchy and people of Cyprus were careful not to provoke the Turkish government, the Turkish authorities nevertheless felt that the position of the Archbishop and the Greek clergy was too powerful now when that same clergy was leading Greeks against the Turks in the War of Independence. Accordingly, in 1821 the usual massacre took place. Archbishop Kyprianos and the other bishops were executed. After this, although there was no Greek revolt in Cyprus, due to the changed circumstances arising from Greek independence and tension between independent Greece and Turkey, the Church in Cyprus could never play the same part under the Turks as it had played before. Politically, it lost ground during the remaining period of Turkish rule in Cyprus and during the British period which followed after 1878. It would not be unfair to say that it rose again into full prominence after the Second World War.

Objectively speaking, the whole British period in the history of Cyprus (1878–1959) is occupied by the struggle of the Orthodox Church for union (*enosis*) with the Greek motherland from which Cyprus had been separated for nearly 800 years. This is essential in order to understand the fundamentally political role of the Church and can be understood when viewed against the background of the decline and dissolution of Ottoman Turkey and Greek successes in Crete, the war of 1912 and the First World War. As has been made clear, the Church of Cyprus had been endowed with a certain political dignity in Byzantine times and had secured unique privileges in that it had won for itself full autocephalic status. Thereafter it had to endure a long period of western rule and oppression, which sharpened its political instinct for survival. Under the Roman Empire it had to play a political part because this was the way in which the Ottoman Empire regulated its relations with its Christian subjects: the Christian clergy were the only recognized political leaders of the Christian population. Naturally, given such a tradition, it is not surprising that the Greek War of Independence was led by the Church. After the British occupation Cyprus was the first apostolic Orthodox Church to be freed of Turkish rule while the other apostolic Orthodox churches remained still in *partibus infidelium*. This ancient dignity and political function of the Church of Cyprus were misunderstood and ignored by the British authorities. It is obvious that the British, in the light of recent events, have never understood how

47

it is possible for a Christian church to engage in political activities. Sir Harry Luke himself points out this difference, providing the following quotation from a Greek newspaper from the time of the First World War:

'In regions where races clash and unredeemed populations struggle against a foreign yoke, a bishop must have nothing of the priest about him except his robes. Unless he combines the courage of a soldier with the guile of a diplomatist and fitness for high command, he may be a saint but he is no fit pastor of militant nationalists. So long as the Near East is not delimited according to right and according to race, saintliness is a positive defect unless it is corrected by the masterfulness of a ruler.'[7]

Despite an apparent understanding of this historical situation Sir Harry Luke cannot prevent himself from attacking the Orthodox Church of Cyprus for participating in politics and, in particular, the role of Archbishop Makarios since 1950. It seems that these efforts of the Church were to be condemned only because they were directed against Britain. Historically speaking they were correct and gentlemanly when applied against the Lusignans and Turks. Sir Harry Luke goes on to quote with approval a statement made in 1956 in the House of Lords by the then Archbishop of Canterbury, Lord Fisher, who said that he viewed Archbishop Makarios 'not as a churchman upholding a religious principle but as a politician calculating risks and chances'. Sir Harry Luke comments on this statement in the following words: '. . . that statement could surprise none familiar with the nature and historical development of the Orthodox Church in the Ottoman Empire and its successive states'. Even so, Sir Harry Luke and other

1 Makarios (then Michael Mouskos) with two other novices of Kykko Monastery, 1936

2 Makarios as a postgraduate student in Boston (U.S.A.)

3   The Archbishop with his parents and brother

4   The Archbishop during his exile in 1956

writers, despite their expert knowledge, go on to attack the Church of Cyprus.

In conclusion it can be stated that the history of the Greek Orthodox faith in Cyprus has not been different from the history and faith of other Hellenic Greek Orthodox churches. History and geography combined to expose the Hellenic world to Moslem assault, first from the Arabs and then from the Turks. The Turkish assault conquered and absorbed all the ethnically Greek territories and held them from the 11th–19th century. Turkish rule itself, in many cases indirect and tolerant, made the Orthodox churches political entities, because this was a Moslem view of society. In these circumstances, in addition to being endowed with political capacity by the Turkish rulers, the Orthodox churches among the Greeks became the guardians of their traditions, culture and language. It must be remembered that for hundreds of years the Greeks, whether of Greece itself or of Cyprus, had been what is termed 'a submerged nationality', that is for generations the map showed only the Ottoman Empire where the Greeks lived. It was the Church which preserved their cohesion and ensured the survival of the Greek community everywhere. The political unity of the Greeks in one Greek state had, over the centuries, become as much a tenet of the Orthodox faith as the divinity of Christ. Only people totally ignorant of history in its wider sense fail to understand that the East is not the West and must obey its own harmonic laws; Cyprus was no exception to this course, the British Empire notwithstanding.

PART B

IV
Britain, Cyprus and the Ottoman Empire

Although Cyprus had been a comparatively late British imperial acquisition (1878), its withdrawal from British rule has caused more trouble and bitterness than similar developments in other regions in countries larger and more populous than Cyprus and which had been under British rule for a longer period of time. The American War of Independence has now been completely forgotten. The independence of India, Pakistan, Burma and Ceylon did not provoke a storm in the Press, neither did the independence of far larger and more populous African territories. There seems to be a 'special relationship' between Britain and the East and this fact has bedevilled any rational approach to the problem of British presence in Egypt, Palestine and the Arab countries in general, not only among the laity but also among those whom one would have expected to be above such prejudices. It now remains to examine this particular situation of Britain in the East.

In the beginning there is a deep-rooted prejudice of the Latin West for the Greek East, born of centuries of religious bigotry. Next in chronological order the East, in addition to being Greek or 'schismatic', became also Moslem and the West chose it for its first aggressive expansion outside its own area during the crusading movement. England was at the heart of this crusading movement. The crusading king, Richard the Lionheart, is the hero of every English schoolboy, particularly since the 19th century encouraged the cult of the hero. The Crusades failed in their endeavour to win back Jerusalem and break Moslem power in the East; they succeeded, however, in smashing the Byzantine Empire and occupying its territories including Cyprus. From the time of the Crusades, therefore, Britain saw itself playing a particular role in the Middle East, suffering in common with another crusading nation, France, from what can be termed as crusading sickness, a recurrent disease, malignant bouts of which occurred in those countries in 1919 and 1956. Of course, 19th century romanticism, the forerunner of nationalism and imperialism, helped to refurbish this crusading tradition which made the East a desirable acquisition.

Then there are also aspects of more material connections such as trade and power politics. For many centuries most of European trade was with the East and England, as a principal trading nation, came to dominate the Eastern market more and more. Furthermore, the British imperial position in India, even before the construction of the Suez Canal, made the Near East an area of vital strategic importance to Britain. Hereafter geography and technical progress seemed to conspire to weld Britain more and more to the Middle East. When geography is mentioned, of course, a glance at the map is sufficient to show that the whole Middle Eastern area, once dominated by the Byzantine Empire, and in the 19th century by the Ottoman, constitutes the meeting place of three continents; it is the true centre of the world. Naturally the great power of Russia to the north of this area casts a long shadow across this sphere of vital British interests, and a true clash of empires developed with Britain trying to preserve its links with India in the

East, and with Russia thrusting across the body of the decrepit Ottoman state towards the Mediterranean and the Persian Gulf. In this contest Britain acquired in the Middle East, Aden in 1839, Cyprus in 1878, Egypt in 1882, Palestine, Jordan, Iraq, and Kuwait in 1919, as well as various British possessions in South Arabia and in the Persian Gulf. In addition the discovery of oil in the Persian Gulf, together with the perfection of the internal combustion engine, has made such a highly technological country as Britain almost entirely dependent on Middle Eastern oil. Thus, history, sentiment and economic interests are all blended in the approach of the British public and their leaders to the problems of the eastern Mediterranean. Britain arrived in the Middle East in 1878 on a new crusade to restrain Tsarist imperialism and she ended by conducting a Turkophile operation (which was only terminated, not by British but by the Young Turk Revolutionaries, in 1908) and suppressing Arab nationalism, Jewish Zionism, and Greek nationalism in Cyprus. This heritage is by no means dead today and the events leading to the termination of the British rule in Cyprus are a testimony to this fact. This attitude prevented successive British governments from coming to a clear-cut decision as to the policy towards Cyprus. It has also prevented them from coming to an understanding with responsible and mature political forces in the island.

The British acquisition of Cyprus in 1878 was the logical outcome of nearly a century of British anti-Russian policy which strove to erect a barrier against Russia along a line stretching from the north-west frontier of India to the Balkans. The support of Turkey, the traditional enemy of Russia, was the basis of this policy and, indeed, had to be so. Britain had saved Turkey from Napoleon and Mohammed Ali, had fought beside Turkey in the Crimean War and, in 1878, had rallied to the aid of Turkey when the Russian armies had reached Constantinople. Cyprus was the obvious reward for Britain for her exertions on behalf of the Sultan (and herself) and, obviously, Britain needed a base in the eastern Mediterranean if she were to be of any use to Turkey militarily. Cyprus, a convenient island, seems to have fulfilled this purpose, but it was never tested as a base because four years later, in 1882, Britain found herself in occupation of Egypt and the Suez Canal. Egypt and the Canal, of course, were much better suited to fulfil the requirements of what is understood by a base—a large country producing a variety of useful crops with a large population and cheap labour, great ports and harbours, two coastlines, the river Nile leading into Africa, and the Canal itself.

Any British force required for action in the Middle East or India could be conveniently assembled in Egypt and any British force from India required for action in the Middle East could do likewise, as was the case in both world wars. Consequently, even before the First World War, Cyprus lost the significance for Britain which had prompted its acquisition. It became just an off-shore island dependent on British-dominated Egypt as it had been in the days of the Ptolemies. After the First World War Britain obtained Palestine and, to the east, Jordan and Iraq, together with various territories in the Persian Gulf, while Britain's crusading sister, France, returned to set up crusading kingdoms in the Levant, now called the Republics of Lebanon and Syria.

Nevertheless, British sentiment was aroused by Cyprus and Palestine much more than by any other British possessions in the Middle East, however important and wealthy these were. The reasons for this were religious and sentimental—namely, memories of the exploits of the Crusaders. For instance, the first British High Commissioner carefully chose the traditional place of Richard the Lionheart's camp, a mile west of Nicosia, as the site for the Government House, which drew the following comment from Hepworth Dixon, a member of his staff:

'Our policy, Sir Garnet, should connect our ancient occupation with the new. Whether we will or not, the facts of our former visit stare us in the face. There, for example, you are building your new quarters on the ground once occupied by Lionheart's men. Richard! Victoria! By these great names we link our second advent with our first. A chain from Richard to Victoria seems long; but England is an ancient country, and her sovereigns are connected with each other by unbroken lines.'[1]

This plainly shows that the identification with the Crusaders played an important part in the psychological make-up of the occupiers. Indeed, Disraeli who was responsible for the whole venture was the author of *Tancred*, sub-titled 'The New Crusade', and it was not long before the new masters of Cyprus were draping around them crusader cloaks and play-acting the parts of the Knights of the Order of St. John who had their H.Q. in medieval crusading Cyprus at Kolossi, after the fall of the crusading states in Syria and Lebanon. Likewise in Palestine the extraordinary British involvement in Zionism, and the complications and contradictions arising from it, provided one of the darkest pages in the history of Britain's presence in the East, leading to a dangerous and unstable state of affairs which has persisted till today and remains one of the biggest unsolved problems. Both these issues, Cyprus and Palestine, seem to be unable to draw a rational response from the British government, though, on the contrary, the British have shown themselves capable of sacrificing great material assets in the same area, as control over oil in Iraq, or Kuwait, without any comparable response or raising of temperature accompanied by perfervid public debates.

Strange to relate, despite all this crusading fervour Cyprus continued to remain, from 1878 to 1914, a part of the Ottoman Empire. Cyprus was only a British base where British troops were stationed. Legally the island continued to be a part of the Ottoman Empire, because the agreement which Disraeli reached with the Sultan prevented despoiling Turkey of any territory by her best ally. British presence in Cyprus, therefore, was definitely maintained in favour of Turkey, and the romantic upper-class Englishmen, who went out to Cyprus considering themselves, indeed, to be the new crusaders, were in fact administering the island on behalf of a Moslem sovereign whom their government was pledged to maintain in Cyprus and elsewhere at all costs. It was only the threat of Germany, obliging Britain to come to an understanding with Russia in 1907, that forced the Young Turk Revolutionaries a year later, in 1908, to break with the no longer reliable British and turn to Germany. The consequence of this Anglo-Turkish divorce was the participation of Turkey, under Young Turk leadership, in the war at the side of Germany against Britain and Russia. With Turkey's entry into the war Britain declared Cyprus to be no longer a part of the Ottoman Empire. With Turkish defeat in the First World War, Turkey acknowledged this fact in the Treaty of Lausanne in 1923. Two years later, in 1925, Cyprus was formally declared a Crown Colony, though by this time, with Germany eliminated and Russia again dangerous because Bolshevik, Britain was again moving towards an accord with the new Turkish regime of Kemal Atatürk; all this boded ill for the aspirations of the Greek Cypriots.

This turn of events was a very sorry sequel to the story of Anglo-Greek relations during the First World War, when Britain offered Cyprus to Greece in order to induce Greek participation in the war on the side of the Allies. Greek failure to respond to this offer has been responsible for the future course of events in Cyprus, and dealt a most severe blow to the idea of *enosis*. Moreover, the defeat of the Turks in the First World War, without much Greek participation, absolved Britain of any obligations towards its less than enthusiastic Hellenic ally. This unfortunate situation was capped by the rash policy of a new regime in Greece: to obtain by arms concessions from the Turkey of Kemal Atatürk, which they had been reluctant to do from the Turkey of the Sultans during the war. The defeat of the Greek expedition to Anatolia in 1922 and its consequences constituted a great setback for Greek aspirations in that area. Also the Italian acquisition of Rhodes and the Dodecanese illustrated the price paid by Greece for hesitation during the war and rashness after it.

But, most important of all, the indomitable position of Britain in the Middle East between 1918 and 1939 had placed the British Empire in the position of the vanished Ottoman Empire. Britain was in control of all the former possessions of the Ottoman Empire (except Syria and Lebanon controlled by its ally and crusading partner, France) and it could be said of Turkey itself. Therefore, British power, having succeeded the Ottoman Empire and, for the time being, not faced with any serious threat to its position, was not in need of making concessions to anyone or looking out for allies. The British hold on Cyprus was likely to continue.

V
Revolt of the Greeks; Modern Greek Nationalism

The Modern Greek State which emerged in 1830 was the first successor state of the Ottoman Empire. From that date onwards the mighty empire of the Ottomans crumbled and began to disintegrate until, after the First World War, the Anatolian homeland became the Republic of Turkey. Greek nationalism, therefore, was both the product and the cause of the 19th century disintegration of the Ottoman Empire; it was nurtured on a ceaseless struggle (sometimes successful and sometimes unsuccessful) to liberate Hellenic people and their territory from Turkish rule.

The first blows aimed at the Ottoman Empire in Europe came in the 18th century due to the continued efforts of Russia and Austria. In 1770 there took place in the Peloponnese the first Greek revolt against the Turks. This revolt had been instigated by Russian agents and was unsuccessful. However, the result of that round in the war between Russia and Turkey was the famous Treaty of Küchük Kainarji in 1774, which gave Russia a foot in the door of the Ottoman Empire, through which they were to apply relentless pressure which finally disintegrated it. In 1798, 25 years and two revolutions later (the American and the French) the Ottoman Empire was attacked in its African and Asiatic possessions by Napoleon and the whole world saw that the Turks were unable to defend themselves without outside (British) help. The result of these blows showed itself in the successful revolts of both Moslem and Christian chieftains against the Sultan—Mohammed Ali in Egypt, Ali Pasha in north-western Greece and Karageorge in Serbia. Actually Karageorge and his Serbians were the first to wrest some autonomy from the Sultan, but the remoteness of Serbia and the confusion of the Napoleonic Wars caused these events to pass unnoticed. The next storm broke out in Greece, and its causes were obvious. Russia, the enemy of Turkey and the protector of the Balkan peoples, was the great victor of 1815, while the growth of romanticism among the educated classes in Britain and France made these countries sympathetic to any form of Greek struggle. Greek merchants and scholars active in Russia and France, such as Adamantios Koraës, had prepared public opinion to be receptive and sympathetic to any movement among the Greeks under Turkish rule by appealing to the classical heritage of Greece.

In Russia, on the other hand, Greek aristocrats (Phanariot families from Rumania) had reached high office at the court of the Tsar. Alexander Capodistrias was Russian Foreign Minister while Prince Alexander Ypsilantes was a general in the Russian Army. In March 1821 he invaded Rumania from Russia in order to raise the Greeks and all the Balkan peoples against the Turks. Although this Russian romantic adventure had failed, a much grimmer blow was struck in Greece itself in April 1821, when the Church in Greece roused the people of the Peloponnese to come out and massacre the Turks.

The rising in the Peloponnese, though travelling along a parallel track to the efforts of Greek expatriate aristocrats and intellectuals, and being politically connected with them, had very different roots. The Greek peasants, merchants, sailors, fishermen, smugglers and bandits who rallied round the banner of the Church in the monasteries of the Peloponnese were no well-born romantics inspired by the myth of ancient Greece. They had been encouraged by the fatal weakness of the Ottoman Empire, as demonstrated for them by the career of Ali Pasha in their midst, and by a blind religious fanaticism which made them rally round the call of the Church and massacre any Turks who fell into their hands. The Turks had now on their hands a full-scale Greek national and religious rebellion. This rebellion was entirely the work of the Church and was led by priests in its initial stages. The structure of the Greek community under the Ottoman Empire, which had been imposed on the Greeks by the Turks themselves, made the Orthodox clergy the political leaders of that community and the chief guardians of the Greek language, and national sentiment fused indissolubly with the Orthodox faith. Here was the perfect example of the Church militant where the natural duty of the priests and bishops was political and even military activity. This was and has continued to be the function of the Orthodox Church in all the successor states of the Ottoman Empire whether independent or under some other foreign occupation. Only outside the Hellenic countries in Orthodox states which had always been independent, such as Russia, the Orthodox Church had no political part to play.

The significant fact that the Turks recognized their enemy as Church-inspired nationalism among the Greeks was borne out by the executions of the Patriarch of Constantinople, the Archbishop of Cyprus and other Greek bishops in Cyprus and elsewhere. These executions were carried out in order to cow the Greeks, and were successful in preventing the Greek revolt from spreading. Otherwise the fire from the Peloponnese might have swept through Constantinople, western Anatolia, and Cyprus. The net result was that the new Greek state was a small area no larger than the Peloponnese. Most of the Greeks continued living under Ottoman rule, or, in the case of the Ionian Islands, under British rule. The whole subsequent history of modern Greece and of Greek nationalism was the struggle with Turkey to liberate Greek territory in Thessaly, Epirus, Macedonia, Thrace, Crete and the other islands. This struggle reached its climax in the Balkan War of 1912–13, which deprived Turkey of the remnants of her empire in Europe (except Constantinople). In 1864 Britain, of her own free will, transferred the Ionian Islands to Greece, while only 14 years later, in 1878, she acquired another Greek island, Cyprus, in circumstances already described. In view of the relationship between Britain and Greece it was generally expected that Britain would do with Cyprus, at a future date, what she had done with the Ionian Islands.

The fact that Cyprus was one more Hellenic land under Turkish rule to be liberated was a sentiment well in evidence in Greece at that time. Nationalistic Greek opinion in Cyprus believed in this as well. Archbishop Sofronios, welcoming the first British High Commissioner, Sir Garnet Wolseley, said:

'We hope, therefore, that from now on a new life begins for the people of Cyprus; a new great period, which will become memorable in the annals of the island. We hope that all shall be instructed without distinction of race or creed, that law is the king of all; that all shall have equal rights and equal responsibility before the law, for equality of rights implies also equality of responsibility; that all shall be used to treading the good road, that is to say, the road of truth, of duty and liberty.'[1]

The most prominent Cypriot historian adds that it is almost axiomatic among Greek historians that Archbishop Sofronios included in his address of welcome the following:

'We accept the change of Government inasmuch as we trust that Great Britain will help Cyprus, as it did the Ionian Islands, to be united with Mother Greece with which it is naturally connected.'[2]

The fact was that Britain was again ruling over Greeks in an age of growing Greek nationalism, and in Cyprus she was now faced with an extremely ancient and venerable Orthodox Church, which enjoyed an extremely high prestige and had acquired a great deal of self-confidence during the period of Ottoman rule, as outlined in previous chapters. The Church concentrated even more during the British period on its task of preserving Hellenism and soon became the standard bearer of the *enosis* orientation of the Cypriots. Cypriot consciousness of being separated from Greece resulted in a great number of volunteers flocking to Greece during the Balkan War of 1912–13 to participate in the struggle against the Turks.

The abolition of the rights of the Ottoman Empire over Cyprus during the First World War, and the transformation of the island into a Crown Colony, combined with the poor stand made by the Greek government over the British offer of *enosis* in 1916, created an atmosphere of bitter disappointment in Cyprus. The Cypriots felt that they had been cheated. The Orthodox Church was

5 The popular reception of the Archbishop at Athens on his return from exile

6 The Archbishop in Athens with the late Greek Foreign Minister, Sofoclis Venizelos

7   Television interview at London Airport before the signing of the London Agreement, 15th February, 1959. *From left to right,* Bishop Anthimos of Kition and the Abbot of Kykko Monastery, Chrysostomos

heading for a head-on collision with the British authorities. The political situation could never be the same as it had been before, and only a new international crisis was needed for battle to be joined.

VI
Religion and Politics in Cyprus under Britain in Respect of 'Enosis'

The British occupation of Cyprus in 1878 was welcomed by both the Greek and Turkish population of the island. The reasons for this are not hard to guess. The Ottoman Empire was in an advanced state of dissolution and its future was dark. Financial oppression in Cyprus was only paralleled by lawlessness and misrule. The Ottoman Empire had to pay for the struggle with Mohammed Ali of Egypt, the Crimean War and the last war with Russia in 1877–8. Everybody was hoping to escape from these intolerable financial burdens; there was evidence that the island of Cyprus was becoming depopulated. The Greek Christian element, however, had another reason to welcome the arrival of the British. The distinguished historian of Cyprus, D. Alastos, says in his book *Cyprus in History* the following: 'Britain was not only a Christian land and a great democratic country but also was, to the Cypriots, that phil-Hellenic power which fifteen years earlier had voluntarily ceded the Ionian Islands to Greece.'

Indeed, Gladstone's gesture of adding the Ionian Islands to Greece in 1864 was the precept which inspired all these sentiments. The statement of Archbishop Sofronios, already mentioned, was very clear. It can be said that the association of the Church of Cyprus with the cause of *enosis* began there and then, and was not a novelty inspired by ambitious Athens politicians and Communist agitators, as subsequently alleged by so many in the British press and Parliament.

It must be observed that Britain was not in a very good position to hand over Cyprus to Greece as Cyprus was not hers to do so. The island was still a part of the Ottoman Empire and the British administration was only introduced by a Convention with the Sultan; Turkey was in fact still the landlord. On the other hand, the fact that Cyprus was still nominally a province of the Ottoman Empire strengthened the terms of the Convention: Britain was obliged to maintain the existing *status quo* including the privileged position of the Church. The Church had started a Greek educational revival in Cyprus dating from the 1740's. This policy culminated in the establishment of the Pancyprian Gymnasium, until 1939 the highest educational establishment in the island, by Archbishop Kyprianos, murdered by the Turks in 1821. This school, naturally, became associated with Greek nationalism and Greek educational influences coming from Athens after the establishment of Greek independence. Such was the state of affairs in the latter Ottoman Empire that the Turks had to tolerate this policy and thus it came about that, under the guidance of the Church, the educational system of Cyprus was modelled on that of Greece, going as far as to copy the curricula and textbooks and to subordinate its schools in some respects to the Ministry of Education in Athens. Great Britain succeeded to this state of affairs, and by its Treaty with Turkey entered into obligations to maintain it. Cyprus thus became the only part of the British Empire officially connected to a foreign country, and this educational connection with Greece, maintained by the Church, was already in 1878 the springboard for undesirable Greek national feeling in Cyprus.

There is no doubt that the Church and the leaders of the Greek community in Cyprus looked on the British occupation of the island as a transient affair—a liberation from Ottoman tyranny leading to union with Greece. This feeling was reciprocated by many in Britain. In 1881, for instance, Gladstone, Prime Minister for the third time, in a telegram to the High Commissioner of the island, expressed his complete sympathy with Greek aspirations and advanced the fact that Cyprus was still an integral part of the Ottoman Empire and the sole obstacle to the union of the island with Greece.

Unfortunately, however, the delay in satisfying national aspirations had the effect of turning the Church in Cyprus against the British government of the island far more than could have been anticipated, and far more than it could have been to Ottoman rule. The reasons for this are not surprising, namely the greater efficiency and strength of Britain. British administration in Cyprus, together with the introduction of the English language, presented a far greater threat to Hellenic nationalism and all that the Church stood for than all the previous foreign regimes in Cyprus taken together. It acted as if a red rag to a bull. The Greek language under British rule expressed Greek national policy far more than it could ever have done during the period of Turkish rule when the Church had practical, political and administrative power in its hands.

In the changed conditions under British rule the defence of the Greek language was felt to be the defence of the last link binding Cyprus to the Hellenic motherland. Therefore it is not surprising that the first confrontation between the Church of Cyprus and the new British rulers of the island occurred precisely on the language question. This is significant because it is necessary to understand that in the world of submerged and emerging nationalities represented in eastern Europe and the Balkans by the Ottoman, Austrian, and the Russian Empires, the national language was the dominant factor in the formation of national consciousness. The history of nationalism in eastern Europe and the Balkans has often been the history of the national language question. The threat to the supremacy of the Greek language in Cyprus placed the island fairly and squarely in the camp of struggling nationalities.

It must be firstly admitted that the British government had no machiavellian aspirations to undermine the position of the Church and the Greek language in Cyprus in order to demoralize its Cypriot subjects. What was at stake was that in the British view the Orthodox Church, and Greek education and the Greek language connected with it, was a monument to superstition and a bar to the progress of all knowledge. Many of the British officials must have felt as St. Paul had felt in Athens when he declared: 'There is much superstition in this place', and had only the interest of the Greek Cypriot population at heart—as they saw it. They honestly believed that Cyprus needed modern education and that that education could only be English and conducted in English. An Englishman, the Rev. J. Spencer, was made Director of Education in Cyprus in 1880, and thus gave great offence to the Church which regarded education as its own special preserve, viewing any interference as a direct attack on the Greek language and Greek national feeling of which it was the guardian. Thus battle was joined right from the outset of the British rule in Cyprus around the most neuralgic point of the Greek Cypriot anatomy. All this could have been expected because English in Cyprus was a greater threat to Greek than Turkish had ever been for the simple reason that English was a far more important language than Turkish, and English officials in Cyprus, being ignorant of Greek and Turkish, had to promote the knowledge of English in order to make themselves understood. Consequently a desire for the knowledge of English was promoted in all aspiring Cypriots, which was seen by the Church as de-Hellenization.

But, above all, the clash between Britain and the Orthodox Church in Cyprus came about due to the fact that under British rule the Church had lost its privileged political position which it had enjoyed under Ottoman rule. Therefore, the Church had no alternative but to adopt an attitude of opposition to Britain and put itself at the head of the struggle for *enosis* which from that day on remained the unswerving political goal. *Enosis*, therefore, that is the union of all people outside Greece with the revived Greek State, has been the aim of the Church of Cyprus for a very long time. In this struggle the nationalist aspirations of the Cypriot leaders were aided by the course of nationalism in the Balkans and the Near East which has been escalating since the end of the 19th century and has by no means yet reached its limits.

The Balkans had been in a state of turmoil ever since the defeat of Turkey by Russia in 1878. The Congress of Berlin in the same year, although it halted for the time being the disintegration of the Ottoman Empire, could not reverse the tide of history. While the Bulgarian crisis was occupying the Powers, Crete which had been left out of the Berlin settlement became a burning question between Greece and Turkey. The Cretan crisis was of long duration, beginning in the 1880's, leading to the Greco-Turkish war of 1897, being solved only by the victory of the Balkan League over Turkey in 1912. The Greek victory of 1912 coincided with the solution of the

Episcopal question in Cyprus, which had paralysed the Church for the best of ten years.[1] Speaking now with a united voice the Church of Cyprus demanded union with Greece. Even before the war had started in 1911 the Archbishop and the Greek members of the Legislative Council addressed the following resolution to the island's High Commissioner:

'Forming as we do, Your Excellency, an inseparable portion of the Greek race, it is natural that we should feel, in a strong and irresistible manner, the desire that our fatherland should be annexed to the Hellenic Kingdom. The fulfilment of this, our aspiration, we base on the strength of our rights and the magnanimity of the English nation. But we will be sorry if it be supposed that these aspirations prevent us from co-operating with the government for the promotion of the manifold moral and material interests of the country.'[2]

The refusal of the government to accept the above resolution forced all the Greek members to resign from the Legislative Council in April 1912. It was following this episode that hundreds of islanders left Cyprus to fight, and many of them to die, in the Greek ranks in the war with Turkey which followed. The victory of the Balkan allies over the Turks, and the consequent enlargement of the national Greek territory, including the final liberation of Crete, marked the high watermark of the old Greek nationalism which began with the Revolution of 1821 and burst out in Anatolia in 1922. This period includes the First World War and its aftermath, which was a period in which many basic attitudes were formed and many great opportunities missed.

The Balkan Wars of 1912–13 were a prelude to the

First World War, which brought about a curious up-heaval in established relationships. Britain and Turkey found themselves on opposing sides and at war. The result was that, after the Turkish declaration of war on Britain, the British declared Cyprus to be no longer part of the Ottoman Empire. On the other hand, Greece, because of the German connections of the royal family, opted for a policy of strict neutrality and refused to contemplate the renewal of war against Turkey, now the ally of Germany, even for the sake of Constantinople and Asia Minor. Britain, France and Russia required Greek help very much due to the defeat of Serbia and Rumania and the participation of Bulgaria on the German side. As the Allies had already mortgaged Constantinople to Russia by a second treaty made in 1915, the British government tried to induce Greek participation in the war by the offer of Cyprus. The Archbishop of Cyprus was to play a vital part in the plan by landing from a British warship in Athens and proclaiming the union of his native island and Greece. The opportunity was missed due to diplomatic hesitation and the miscalcula-tion of the Greek government at that time. Consequently Greek entry into the war on the side of the Allies was no longer connected with *enosis* for Cyprus. The last oppor-tunity to achieve an equitable solution of the national demands of the Cypriots was missed in 1919 when Venizelos was the Prime Minister of Greece (and at the height of his popularity) and Lloyd George who, after Gladstone, was the most phil-Hellenic Prime Minister in British history, were attending the Paris Peace Confer-ence. Venizelos was assured that when the Greek ques-tion was formally solved Cyprus would be united with Greece, and Lloyd George in a letter to a Cypriot Mission in London, stated that he was 'fully aware of the sentiment which exists among the Greek population of

Cyprus for union with Greece' and then added: 'The wishes of the inhabitants of Cyprus will be treated with the most careful and sympathetic consideration by H.M. Government when they consider its future.'[3]

At the same time Archbishop Cyrillos III was pressing in person, at the head of the delegation, the demand for *enosis* on the British government in London. The address which the Archbishop handed over to Lord Milner, Secretary for the Colonies, contains the following sentiments:

> '... fulfilling the sacred mandate of our ... native country, we have come to the Metropolis of the Empire to respectfully submit to the government ... our just claim that the principles for which the democratic peoples have fought and bled be applied also to Cyprus, by the return of the island to Hellas. ... The severance, on 5th November, 1914, of the last link with the Turks by the abolition of the Treaty of 1878 while it increased our joy, strengthened our convictions that a national rehabilitation was thus rendered easier. ... Nor can we recollect without feelings of deep gratitude to Great Britain, her generous recognition of our national aspirations and rights by the offer made in 1915 of our native island to Greece.'[4]

The outcome of this Mission was failure and, in the frustration that set in as a result, the Greek members resigned from the Legislative Assembly. The government of Cyprus responded with marshal law and served warning on leading *enosists* that they would be deported. Finally, the Greek disaster in Asia Minor in 1922 and the subsequent fall of Lloyd George in Britain removed any hope of a peaceful solution of what was to become the

Cyprus question. What was ignored at the time was the intense passion which the issue of *enosis* was now arousing in Cyprus though almost 10 years more were to elapse before violence was to erupt.

In 1925 Cyprus was declared to be a Crown Colony, which dashed the hopes of *enosis* and confirmed the Church in its position of hostility towards the British rule of the island. A political force, the National Organization, came into being, dedicated to utilizing all possible means to achieve union with Greece. The Archbishop was the President and his bishops were in charge of the district organizations. Thus the Church became fully involved in a political struggle, and it did not hesitate for a moment to place itself at the head. An outburst came in 1931, after another rejection (by a Labour government) of a plan for constitutional advance, and in conditions of mounting economic crisis. The government imposed a Tax Bill, rejected by the Legislative Council, and the Greek members of the Legislative Council decided to initiate a policy of civil disobedience. On 17th October, 1931, the Bishop of Kition read a manifesto in which he advocated the overthrow of British rule. On 20th of the same month the same Bishop appealed in public for a revolution and the Greek members resigned from the Legislative Council. Riots broke out in Nicosia and in various parts of the island, led in most cases by the clergy carrying Greek flags. The Government House in Nicosia was burned with all the Governor's possessions and six people were killed.

The *enosis* riots of 1931 could be cited as the starting point of a violent movement in Cyprus, led by the Church, and made the name of *enosis* familiar to the world. More than 2,000 persons were convicted in connection with the riots and the leaders, including the Bishops of Kition and Kyrenia, were exiled. The Legislative Council was suppressed and the Colony was henceforth ruled by decree. The exile of two bishops made the consecration of a new Archbishop impossible following the death of Archbishop Cyrillos in 1933, and from that year until 1947 the Church of Cyprus was administered by the only bishop of the island, namely Bishop Leontios of Paphos, acting as *locum tenens*. The Church under his leadership never abandoned the policy of *enosis*, though it was gravely handicapped by having no head and by the oppressive policies of the government. Also the darkening international situation, leading to the Second World War, led to a neutralization, for the time being, of the struggle for *enosis*; the political aspirations behind it, far from being crushed were simply driven underground which made them ripe for a radical transformation after 1945. And, when the issue of *enosis* was to be raised again after the Second World War, the Church was again in the lead, thus proving that no political solution could ever be found to this problem without the participation and blessing of the Church. The denial of *enosis* to the people of Cyprus served indirectly to strengthen the political hold of the Church.

VII
The Emergence of Makarios

On the eve of the Second World War Cyprus was again governed by despotism. Since 1931 the people of Cyprus had lost all the privileges which they had enjoyed during the Ottoman rule and the early British administration. They were now merely a colony, sundered for ever, so it seemed, from their fellow Greeks, and with no say in their own affairs. The British government prevented the election of a new Archbishop after 1933 by the expedient of not allowing the exiles of 1931 to return, and by prohibiting prelates from other Orthodox churches to come to Cyprus in order to convene the electoral Synod and supervise the election of a new Archbishop.

The outbreak of the Second World War in 1939 did not affect the situation materially and Cyprus was far from the battlefields of that war. A year later the situation changed most dramatically and tragically. Britain was fighting Germany alone. Italy had joined Germany in the war and was attacking Egypt from Libya and, to round off her claims, Mussolini launched an attack against neutral Greece. Thus, once more Britain and Greece found themselves as allies in the common struggle, and in the dark days of the winter of 1940-1, among the mass of German bombs which were devastating many British cities, the embattled Britain was cheered by the unexpected success of the Greek army in its war against the Italian aggressors in the mountains of Epirus. Admiration for Greece and her people, now almost forgotten, knew no bounds. These developments affected radically the whole situation in Cyprus and closed the chapter which began in 1931. Cyprus was in the front line, as in the First World War, against the enemies[1] of Hellenic nationalism. Volunteers flocked to arms, both for the defence of the island and for service outside, and there was a sense of emergency and purpose based on the hope that, now that Britain and Greece were standing shoulder to shoulder as allies, Britain could not forego the offer of the union of Cyprus with Greece. Indeed, early in 1941 Mr. Anthony Eden, as he was then, paid a visit to Athens in his capacity as Foreign Minister and intimated to the Greek government that the British government would be prepared to open discussions on the problem after the end of the war. Nevertheless, after the German invasion of Greece and Crete the British government refused to make Cyprus the seat of the Greek government in exile, and the Governor of Cyprus, though not the British government itself, denied the claim made by the Prime Minister of the Greek government in exile in London that Cyprus was part of post-war Greece.

While these events were taking place the man who was to bear the name which has become inseparable from the history of Cyprus after 1945 was quietly starving in a suburb of Athens.

Somehow one cannot imagine the career of Archbishop Makarios III without the part played in it by the Second World War just as one cannot imagine the end of British rule in Cyprus without the changes brought about in the world-wide position of Britain by that war.

Michael Christodoulos Mouskos, perhaps the most famous occupant of the throne of St. Barnabas since its

77

foundation, was born on 13th August 1913, in the village of Pano Panayia on the southern slopes of the Troodos mountains. His father, like so many people living in that mountainous district, was partly farmer and partly shepherd. The boy was the first-born son of the family and as such grew up, like so many peasant children in Cyprus at that time, helping his father with his field work. However, the village of Pano Panayia was situated in a famous neighbourhood because near it was the monastery of Chrysoroyiatissa, while the clock tower of the famous monastery of Kykko, some 15 miles away, was visible from the village. The boy thus literally grew up within the shadow cast by the towers of one of the most famous monasteries in the Orthodox world.

Although the young Michael had been destined by his father to follow him in his trade as shepherd, he was greatly influenced by the religious environment in which he grew up and by the Church connections in his own family. For instance, his uncle was the priest of the village and the young boy delighted in helping him to clean and repaint the church and in assisting his uncle in preparing for the Mass. He also was a frequent visitor at the Chrysoroyiatissa monastery where he was be-friended by the monks. All this time he was attending the local school, four miles from his home, while during the school holidays he went up with his father to the mountain range to help him with his sheep. It was during these years that the boy Michael conceived a great yearning to become a monk and enter the wonderful monastery of Kykko: he had fallen completely under the spell of one of the most famous and most holy places of Orthodox Christendom.

Mention has already been made of Kykko monastery. It was founded in the 12th century in the last period of Byzantine rule. The story of its foundation is a romantic myth of pride and arrogance, miraculous diseases and miraculous cures—at the same time very Greek and very Christian: an outrage committed by a brave warrior against the person of a holy man was avenged by a mysterious disease, just as the Greeks at Troy were stricken by the plague sent by Apollo because they had laid outrageous hands on one of his priests. The story goes that one day, while hunting in the Troodos mountains, the Byzantine Duke of Cyprus, Michael Voutomedes, became detached from his companions and, losing his way in the forest, sought information in a haughty and arrogant way from one of the hermits who lived in that isolated place. The holy man refused to answer and tried to avoid the Governor, whereupon Voutomedes set about him and beat him soundly. Then the hermit spoke and laid a solemn curse on the arrogant noble. A few days later Voutomedes was struck down by a mysterious disease and was on the point of death. He remembered what had happened in the Troodos forest and had the holy hermit brought to him and promised to perform any penance set by him if only he would pray to heaven to remove the curse of the disease from him. The conditions which the hermit made for curing Voutomedes was that the Governor should procure from the Emperor in Constantinople one of his greatest treasures—a miraculous icon of the Virgin, allegedly painted by St. Luke—and bring it to Cyprus. Voutomedes agreed, was cured, and set out for Constantinople together with the holy man. At Constantinople another cycle of mysterious illness and miraculous cures occurred until the Emperor agreed to send the original miraculous icon to Cyprus. Finally, after many tribulations, the icon of the Virgin by St. Luke arrived in Cyprus, and Voutomedes had a church built to house it near the hermit's cell in the Troodos mountains at

Kykko. This was the origin of Kykko monastery which, because of the miraculous powers of its icon, acquired a fame in the Orthodox world equal to that of the holy mountain of Athos, St. Katherine's monastery in Sinai and the Stoudion monastery in Constantinople. Pilgrims flocked from all over the world to Kykko. The monastery grew in fame and riches, surviving and surmounting such vicissitudes as the Frankish conquest, the Venetians, the Turks, and fires and earthquakes. It acquired great wealth of which a great deal came from Russia where Kykko was held in particular respect: the bells of Kykko were a gift from Russian believers. It was this monastery which young Michael Mouskos entered as a novice at the age of 12 in 1926, having realized his dream at last. He had managed to persuade his father to let him follow his bent and his happiness. His ambition had been fulfilled and, unknown to himself, the turning point in his life had been reached. The boy's persistence in entering Kykko at such an early age was in a way indicative of his character and of the single-minded purpose he has since displayed in his political career.

At the monastery the young novice was given work at the refectory and put in charge of serving the guests of the monastery. He attended to his duties most conscientiously, so much so that sometimes he was late for his lessons at the monastery school for which he was sometimes caned by the Abbot. It was also in the refectory kitchen that the young novice gave vent one day to his first political manifestations by scribbling on the kitchen wall the words *Zeto i Enosis* (Long Live *Enosis*). He also decorated his cell with his initials which are today shown to tourists as one of the great attractions of that famous monastery. It was, perhaps, in his monastic cell at Kykko that the future Archbishop, applying all the strength of his intellect to a single task, developed his most typical characteristic, that of patience and impassiveness in the face of difficulties and crises, which has stood him so well in the tempestuous career of his political life.

The qualities of the young novice did not pass unnoticed by the Abbot of Kykko. He realized that in young Michael there was material for greater things than could be accomplished within the walls of a monk's cell. The cloister had done its work. The time came for Michael Christodoulos Mouskos to broaden his intellect now that his character had been formed, and he was dispatched by the Abbot to terminate his studies at the Pancyprian Gymnasium in Nicosia—the most famous school in Cyprus which was the gateway for all Cypriots to universities in Greece, England, the United States and elsewhere.

At the Gymnasium the young novice distinguished himself by the same industry and single-mindedness of purpose which he had displayed at Kykko. He was quiet and collected, and applied himself above all to perfecting his style. This is Makarios the pupil as remembered by his classmate and now his personal doctor, who also recalls that at that time the young Michael wrote poems. Although very reticent now to talk about his poetry, the Archbishop admits that his years at the Pancyprian Gymnasium awakened in him a love of literature and that, apart from the Greek classics, his favourite authors are Goethe and Victor Hugo.

Having finished his secondary education at the Pancyprian Gymnasium, Michael Mouskos was created a deacon, and took the name Makarios under which he has always been known since. His talents were by now so obvious that Cyprus could not offer him anything more and in 1938 at the age of 25 he left his native island for the first time for distant Athens where he was enrolled in the Faculty of Theology at the University. He was far from home, in a strange big city with war clouds gathering on the horizon. The war came to Greece in October 1940 and was followed the next spring by the German invasion of Greece. Deacon Makarios, being a British subject, was in grave danger of being interned by the Germans and decided to return to Cyprus but the ship on which he was due to sail was bombed and sunk by the Germans. After that he had no alternative but to remain in Athens under the German and Italian occupation. He continued his studies at the University as best as he could, graduating in theology and going on to read law while supporting himself by obtaining the post of deacon at St. Irene's Church in a fashionable part of Athens. Many years later the archpriest in charge of St. Irene's Church, Vassilios, remembered Makarios as the most courteous deacon he has ever had under him, and who always attended punctually to his duties. These were equally divided between the altar of St. Irene's and the lecture rooms of the University. It was a hard life in occupied Athens, and many were the days when the student deacon did not have anything to eat. It was a period of trial, and Makarios was only able to surmount it because of his early spartan training at the monastery of Kykko where young men were not used to an easy life. In such circumstances it was not surprising that Makarios in German-occupied Athens did not take part in any resistance activities. He admits today quite openly: 'I was too young and did not have enough strength for it.'

Makarios remained in Athens after the end of the war preparing for his priesthood to which he was characteristically consecrated on 13th January, 1946, at St. Irene's Church in Athens. He then took over a parish of his own in Piraeus. It is interesting to note here that Makarios was now 30 years of age and unmarried. According to usages of the Greek Orthodox Church, priests can only marry before their ordination: they cannot marry afterwards. Those priests who are single by the time of their ordination must remain single, and from their ranks the Orthodox bishops are recruited. Makarios was now set on his way to an episcopal career. However, the road from a working-class parish in Piraeus to the archiepiscopal palace in Nicosia and his position as Head of State was not going to progress according to the traditional rules of the game. Makarios's parish activities in Athens did not last long. To his own great surprise he received a grant from the World Council of Churches to proceed to post-graduate studies in the United States. The desire which sent the boy from Pano Panayia along the road to Kykko was now taking him to the New World and new intellectual and political influences.

His scholarship sent him to the University of Boston in Massachusetts. At first the young priest from Athens found America different and bewildering but he soon settled down and developed a liking for the United States and the American way of life, which is rather surprising for a monk and a Greek Orthodox prelate. He felt so much at home in the United States that he began to think seriously of settling down there in order to pursue his career among the Greek Orthodox community. He also considered returning to and remaining in Athens. He wanted to teach theology at a university. Any return to Cyprus or to the monastic world seemed highly unattractive to him at that time. However, in distant Cyprus a political tide was rising unleashed by the aftermath of the war. The pendulum was swinging against British colonialism, and in Cyprus the issues of 1931 were brought up again. Indeed, the situation was more poignant with dangers than in 1931 because, while Britain's post-war Labour government allowed for the return of the remaining exiles of 1931 and permitted on the whole a more liberal political life, it did not restore to Cyprus its pre-1931 Constitution. In such circumstances the Church, as since immemorial times, found itself in the forefront of the struggle under the banner of *enosis*. It was then that attention was turned to the absentee monk from Kykko who had for years been living and studying abroad. One day early in 1948 Makarios received a telegram in Boston that he had been elected Bishop of Kition. He himself remarked that this must have been the first time in the history of the Church of Cyprus that a student (although a post-graduate one) had been elected bishop. Makarios admits that he was initially upset by this surprise because he had wanted to remain in America and finish his studies. Perhaps this was the reason why he did not immediately return to Cyprus but remained for several weeks more in Boston. Another reason could have been that the clean-shaven Makarios needed that time to grow a beard which is the necessary attribute of every Orthodox prelate, particularly in Cyprus.

On 13th June, 1948, Makarios was consecrated Bishop of Kition in the Cathedral of Larnaca and became, at the same time, secretary of the Ethnarchy, thus becoming the most important political adviser of the Archbishop, a kind of ecclesiastical Prime Minister. He showed his drive and zest almost immediately. Typical of him and his period is the story that when a local politician told him that he was weak because he had no organization or party behind him he replied: 'No, I am strong. And my strength is my love for my people, whom I trust.' His greatest achievement was the organization of the plebiscite of 1950 (15th January) fought on the issue of *enosis.* This plebiscite organized and carried out by the Church produced a 96 per cent majority in favour of ending the colonial status of the island, and uniting with Greece. Makarios, who, as a kitchen helper at Kykko, had scribbled on the wall *Zeto i Enosis,* had now written *enosis* across the whole of Cyprus and, indeed as it turned out, across the whole world, for it was Makarios more than anybody else who made practically everybody in this world acquainted with this word and what it represented.

The issue with Britain had now been joined, and when Archbishop Makarios II, who had been ailing for some time, died there could be only one candidate for the archiepiscopal throne, the young Bishop of Kition who had been the driving force behind the plebiscite of January 1950. He was elected unanimously as Archbishop—something which had never happened in the long history of the Church of Cyprus. On 20th October, 1950, while the attention of the whole world was centred on the war in distant Korea, Makarios was enthroned as Makarios III, Archbishop of Cyprus and Ethnarch. This event marked the turning point in the history of Cyprus and, although it was not known at the time, spelt the end of the British rule of the island. Britain was soon to find in the young Archbishop an opponent of mettle, such as never before encountered in the whole course of her colonial history, and was to prove incapable of dealing with him.

PART C

VIII
The Priest and the Soldier

People of Anglo-Saxon countries, not having for centuries been under foreign occupation, do not know what it means to offer resistance to foreign occupiers, whether that resistance is led by churchmen or lay people. In the conditions of the eastern Mediterranean, as explained previously, resistance against foreign oppressors is part and parcel of the heritage of every community in that area, and the leadership is as often as not supplied by their priests. This is certainly the tradition of the Greek Orthodox Church. The Greek Revolution of 1821 was begun by Archbishop Germanos who had hoisted the standard of revolt and organized and blessed the first battalions of revolutionaries. Archbishop Makarios III found himself in a similar situation: he had to fight for independence against a foreign occupier who still represented quite a powerful force although in process of dissolution; a state similar to that of the Ottoman Empire in 1821. Nor must it be forgotten that as Ethnarch he was also the civil head of his community and indirectly responsible for all its non-ecclesiastical attributes. A situation somewhat similar exists in respect of those lay rulers who exercise ecclesiastical powers, such as the heads of Protestant states, and the Tsar of Russia prior to 1917.

The Archbishop, when he took over his high office,

had to survey the task before him. He had had a resounding success over the plebiscite. British power, it was evident by 1950, was in decline due to the outcome of the Second World War and the rising tide of anti-colonialism. Anti-colonialism, too, was being fed by the existence of the United Nations and its principles: colonial possessions and impositions of foreign rule by force are not compatible with the Charter of the United Nations. Finally after 1950 Greece acquired a stable government due to the defeat of the Communists in the civil war in which Britain had aided Greece. Makarios was quite correct in his analysis that this was the time to reopen the question of *enosis* and to satisfy the age-old aspirations of the people of Cyprus to end their separation from the rest of the Greeks. Makarios announced his policy to the whole world on the very day of his enthronement when he said: 'I shall not rest for a moment in my efforts to see union with Greece achieved.'

Makarios had already been to Greece in 1949 on an *enosis* mission. In 1951 he went there again, and this was the beginning of a long series of travels which took him all over the world as the standard bearer of his self-appointed mission. In 1952 he visited the United States to watch the United Nations at work. Next year he visited Egypt, Syria and Lebanon, Britain, France, Greece, at the beginning of 1954, and then America again, commanding respect everywhere by his presence and raising everywhere the cry for *enosis*, which was beginning to be echoed by Greeks throughout the world. Perhaps the most important mission undertaken by the Archbishop at this stage of the struggle was his unhesitating journey to Bandung in Indonesia in 1955 to attend the anti-colonial conference of Afro-Asiatic countries.

By this one bold strategic stroke he aligned the problem of Cyprus with the problem of anti-colonialism

throughout the world. It was a very imaginative gesture
on his part because Bandung, being an Afro-Asiatic
meeting, was entirely non-European and non-Christian.
The appearance of a European and a Christian and a
bishop at such a meeting showed an imagination and a
broadness of spirit which is not compatible with the
caricature of Makarios as a narrow-minded religio-
political fanatic.

At this time certain people were convinced that Britain
would never release her hold on Cyprus without the
use of violence. The chief among these people was a
retired Greek army officer, Colonel George Grivas, who
himself was of Cypriot origin. He had taken part in
wartime and post-war Greek politics on the extreme
right wing. After the termination of the civil war in
Greece his thoughts turned to his native Cyprus and on
his own admission, as early as 1948, while Makarios
was still a student at Boston, he began discussing plans
for an armed revolution in Cyprus with his collaborators.
In 1950 he had reached an understanding with a group
of Cypriots living in Athens and dispatched one of them
to Cyprus to study the course of the struggle for *enosis*.
The next year Grivas contacted General Cosmas, Chief
of the General Staff, and through him Field Marshal
Papagos who was soon to become Prime Minister of
Greece. In May 1951 Grivas formed a definite group in
Athens consisting of his former brother officers and
Cypriots living in exile in Athens. The aim of this organization was to end British rule in Cyprus by means of an
armed struggle. Later in that year Grivas returned to
Cyprus to visit his brother and carry out a military and
political survey of the island. He soon contacted Archbishop Makarios but found his attitude towards the use
of violence negative. Makarios at this stage was relying
on the Greek government and the United Nations and

Grivas records that the Archbishop's attitude at that time was the only unsatisfactory thing which he had found in Cyprus.[1] In 1952 a second committee for the liberation of Cyprus was organized in Athens under the chairmanship of the Archbishop, though Grivas adds that he doubted at this time whether the Archbishop really wanted a forceful solution. The truth was that Makarios was finding difficulty in influencing the Greek government and the political situation had hardened in Britain, due to the return to power of the Conservative party in the elections of 1951. Makarios at that date wanted a political solution relying on the United Nations, but his political instinct told him to build up something more provocative as a reserve, and he recognized a useful adjunct in Grivas's organization, although his personal attitude to the Colonel, according to the latter's testimony, was one of utmost reluctance.

Later on in the same year, 1952, two important events occurred which had a great bearing on the future. Grivas made a further tour of Cyprus where he made a careful survey of the local youth organizations. He also had further consultations with Makarios which, from his point of view, were very unsatisfactory. Makarios was adamant in his opposition to the use of violence against the British in Cyprus, i.e. he was against the taking of lives, as befitted his priestly office. The most that he would permit was sabotage against installations, etc., which would have a propaganda value without taking a toll of human lives. Grivas, however, saw this as an impractical restriction, unwarranted optimism and humanitarianism. He noted: 'We parted on a note of disagreement.'

The second event which marked a turning point in the story of *enosis* was the Greek general election of November 16th, 1952, which was held while Grivas was negotiating with Makarios. The result of that election brought Field Marshal Papagos to power and gave Greece a strong and popular government. Strange as it may appear, the victory of Papagos postponed for the time being all plans for an armed insurrection in Cyprus. Field Marshal Papagos was determined to make one more appeal to Britain to settle the Cyprus question and, failing that, to place the Cyprus issue before the United Nations. All this accorded very well with the personal inclinations of the Archbishop and indicates his true political preference which was always to avoid bloodshed and to settle any outstanding issues on the basis of negotiations between himself, Greece and Britain, either directly or under the auspices of the United Nations. It is tragic that the policy of the then British government completely thwarted the aspirations of the Archbishop and brought about what he wanted to avoid most of all: a period of violence, which also had the result of diminishing still further Britain's standing in the post-war world.

The inevitable step, so it seems, occurred towards the end of 1953 and defeated the main endeavour of those years—the harnessing of the Greek government to the cause of *enosis* in order to put the Cyprus problem before the United Nations. The veteran Greek soldier Field Marshal Papagos had become Prime Minister but, before his government was going to challenge Britain before the United Nations, he wanted to open direct negotiations over Cyprus. The British Foreign Secretary, Mr. Anthony Eden, made a private visit to Greece and was approached by Field Marshal Papagos over the Cyprus problem. Eden was a sick man and Papagos was no diplomat. Eden's reply to Papagos's question as to any possibility for self-determination for Cyprus was one brutal 'never'. This high-handed and arrogant piece of 19th century treatment stung Papagos to the quick. Papagos said after this interview to Stephanopoulos, Greece's Foreign Minister: 'He told me "never"—not even "we shall see".'[2] This 'never' was responsible for the whole course of subsequent British policy in Cyprus and for all the bloodshed as the consequence of that policy. Eden's 'never' really ended another phase in the history of *enosis*. From now on Makarios, whether he liked it or not, had to face the consequences of an armed struggle and bloodshed.

Events beyond his control now forced the hand of the Archbishop and he was no longer in a position to control desperate men because Eden and the obstinate men in his government and party were destroying the very foundations of the Archbishop's policy to curb violence and to settle the problems of Cyprus by negotiations. In the circumstances, recalling the words of Talleyrand, Eden's 'never' was 'not a blunder but a crime'.

Eden's 'never' has reverberated through history, no doubt due to the prestige of his office and his personality. However, there was a second 'never' in the sorry tale of the first post-war Conservative administration and Cyprus. This time the 'never' was not uttered during an unofficial private conversation, which only came to light some time after, but in broad daylight, so to speak, on the floor of the House of Commons. On the 28th July, 1954, Mr. Henry Hopkinson, the Minister of State for Colonial Affairs, answered certain questions put to him by Mr. James Griffiths and other members of the Labour Opposition in respect of the situation in Cyprus. Griffiths asked about how the new constitutional proposals for Cyprus compared to those framed in 1948. He then proceeded to ask if these new constitutional proposals were to lead in Cyprus to full self-government within the Commonwealth, with full Dominion status (as it then was called), within the meaning of the Statute of Westminster and in conformity with post-war British policy in regard to colonial territories.

Mr. Hopkinson's answer to this question contained the following words:

> 'In regard to the second part of the question, it has always been understood and agreed that there are certain territories in the Commonwealth which, owing to their particular circumstances, can never expect to be fully independent. I think the right honourable gentleman will agree that there are some territories which cannot expect to be that. I am not going as far as that this afternoon, but I have said that the question of the abrogation of British sovereignty cannot arise—that British sovereignty will remain.'[3]

Whereas Eden spoke extempore and with sincerity, the statement made by Mr. Hopkinson was intermingled with promises of Constitution and reforms. The contradictory nature of this declaration amounted to a hypocritical manœuvre, and this was immediately pointed out by several speakers in the House of Commons including Tom Driberg and the late Aneurin Bevan.

There is no doubt that the Hopkinson 'never' dictated the outburst of violence in Cyprus. The extremist elements knew that whatever negotiations Makarios undertook with the British the results would be sterile. The whole bargaining position of the Archbishop was undermined in respect to the hot-heads in his own camp; he could no longer stop or appease them by the prospect of constitutional negotiations with the British government. Thus the Conservative government shattered the influence for moderation and common sense prevailing among Cypriot political leaders. The Archbishop was powerless in face of intransigence on the part of those around Colonel Grivas and now equally of Her Majesty's government. The Hopkinson 'never' did even more damage in the long run to the prospects of a peaceful solution to the Cyprus problem than any ill-tempered remark made by Eden.

Makarios, the Greek government, and all those who desired a peaceful solution had only one more resource, although a slender one, namely an appeal to the United Nations. This was the business of the Greek government and Field Marshal Papagos, who was strongly pro-British, counselled forbearance and patience as he placed all his hopes on some solution being found in New York. This strengthened the hand of Makarios and explains the dampening down of the explosive situation building up in Cyprus. Makarios had one more chance to oppose violence by prevailing on militant elements, represented by Colonel Grivas, to await the outcome of the placing of Cyprus on the agenda of the United Nations.

This is far from the image of Makarios as a firebrand wading through seas of blood. Here is the picture of a man who was risking his whole political future and reputation because he would do anything rather than be responsible for violence, and those who advocated a militant course, such as Colonel Grivas, leave us in no doubt about it.

The last chance to avoid violence in Cyprus occurred in the autumn of 1954. Greece endeavoured to put Cyprus on the agenda of the United Nations Assembly, calling for 'self-determination' for Cyprus. This emphasis on self-determination rather than union with Greece was a shrewd move on the part of Makarios because it was aimed at influencing the growing number of new Afro-Asian countries in the United Nations. A straight declaration in favour of *enosis* would have looked like a piece of annexation. This, however, did not prevent the Archbishop from declaring in a sermon he gave in Nicosia on the eve of the United Nations debate: 'We aim at *enosis* and only *enosis*.'[4]

Here the Archbishop can be accused of steering a contradictory course, but anyone wishing to remain in control of a tense political situation would have to produce something different for home consumption from that which was being offered abroad. This political equivocationalism of the Archbishop has been both the source of his political strength and weakness.

The Greek appeal to the United Nations failed and in the end even the Greek representative voted in favour of a watered-down draft which shelved the whole issue. The Archbishop who had gone for the debate to New York returned to Cyprus in January 1955. He had now no arguments to oppose the advocates of militancy such as Colonel Grivas and his followers. As a matter of fact his prestige had suffered: he had been let down by the Greek government and the United Nations. On the other hand, the outcome was inevitable due to the lack of any action in Cyprus. Grivas recounts that before the United Nations debate, in October 1954, Makarios stopped dithering and started urging him to organize some action in Cyprus in order to impress world public opinion.[5] The reason that no action was possible in Cyprus by Grivas or anybody else until April 1955 had been entirely due to the Archbishop's great reluctance in the past to agree to any action likely to result in violence. Now he saw the necessity for it after having lost the first round. It was to be said at this stage that his mistake was to have been too optimistic and to have put too much hope in the United Nations without adequate preparations in Cyprus.

IX
The Archbishop Hoists the Standard of 'Enosis'

The intransigence of the Conservative government in Britain and the abdication of the Greek government at the United Nations (though there was little chance in 1954 of Cyprus being put on the agenda even if Greece had voted against shelving the issue) made it impossible for Makarios to continue with his political plans without the support of militant elements. This was particularly important because the widespread belief that the Cypriots would refrain from any action could be said to have influenced the British authorities in supposing that they had a far wider margin in Cyprus than in fact they had. The difficult position of Makarios can be imagined if one considers that, once a military struggle started, he in fact lost half his authority which passed into the hands of the military leaders of the movement. This could have been a fatal mistake in the case of a lesser person; Makarios was able to maintain and to recover his prestige during and after the phase of the armed struggle, though in this he was helped by the British all along, first by his deportation in 1956 and subsequently by British hostility towards his regime.

On midnight 31st March, 1955, Grivas and the saboteurs trained by him provided Britain with a memorable fools' day. The first strike consisted entirely of bomb throwing and took the authorities by surprise. From then on the campaign of violence escalated mainly into attacks on the police. The immediate response, however, to E.O.K.A.[1] bombs was another British 'never'. At the end of June, Britain invited the Greek and Turkish governments to send representatives to confer in London on political and defence matters affecting the eastern Mediterranean including Cyprus. The Greek government accepted but appealed again to the United Nations to put the question of Cyprus on the agenda of the Assembly. No invitation was sent to Archbishop Makarios to put the views of the Cypriots at the proposed conference or even to send an observer, while, on the other hand, Britain officially introduced Turkey into a dispute which had hitherto only concerned Britain and Greece alone. Indeed, the Tripartite Conference of August, 1955, was a dextrous manœuvre of which Sir Anthony Eden, now Prime Minister, was the chief architect. Eden knew of the wider differences between the Greeks and the Turks in respect of Cyprus. He himself has recorded: 'It was as well I wrote on a telegram that they (the Turks) should speak out, because it was the truth that the Turks would never let the Greeks have Cyprus.' His tactics were to sit back and let the Greeks and the Turks do all the talking; it now appeared that Cyprus was an issue between Greece and Turkey and not between Greece and Britain, and that Britain was trying to keep the balance between the two.[2]

Britain followed up her Turkish manœuvre by preparing a new constitution for Cyprus which would have excluded *enosis* and maintained British sovereignty over the island as derived from the Treaty of Lausanne (1923). The new British Foreign Secretary, Harold Macmillan, replying to a question put to him by the Turkish Foreign Minister, Zorlu, said that he did not see any prospect of any change in the status of Cyprus 'in the foreseeable future'. He then went on to say: 'We do not accept the principle of self-determination as one of universal application. We think that exceptions must be made in view of geographical, traditional, historical, strategic and other considerations.'[3] The conference ended in failure to achieve any understanding between Britain and Greece on the issue of Cyprus.

In the meantime, in Cyprus, Makarios was faced with the problem of convincing both Britain and Greece that the problem of Cyprus could not be solved by ignoring the wishes of the Cypriots. At the same time he was still trying to keep the E.O.K.A. action within bounds. On the admission of Grivas, Makarios exercised his entire influence to veto any attempt on the life of General Keightley, Commander-in-Chief, Middle East Land Forces. He was completely set against the development of the E.O.K.A. campaign, on which he looked as a form of political pressure, into a full-blown guerrilla campaign. Grivas recalls that on 1st May, 1955, he made the following note after receiving an admonition from the Archbishop: 'The Archbishop's attitude is strange. Is he worried about the financial side of things; is he afraid of losses; or of responsibility for bloodshed? Which of these things? Perhaps it is a matter of pride since he spoke against guerrilla action from the start and did not want to bring in arms necessary for this kind of war. Whatever the reasons, I shall go forward.'[4]

The above is highly indicative of the way in which the situation was developing. The Archbishop had been forced by British intransigence to sanction a limited use of force (sabotage) in order to exercise political pressure. But once force had been resorted to, bringing about the counter-application of force, it grew of its own accord and control over events inevitably passed into the hands of those who had arms. They became an element very difficult to control because, in the conditions of the struggle, everyday decisions were theirs and they were determined, whatever the circumstances, 'to go forward'. As future events were to show it could be argued that by sanctioning military actions under Colonel Grivas, Makarios had created at best a blunt instrument and at worst a frankenstein.

The end of 1955 marked the point of no return. The first thing to be noted was that British security forces had failed to account for E.O.K.A. This was not surprising in the light of the fact that British statesmen had failed to find the type of political solution to disarm those popular instruments which were behind E.O.K.A.'s campaign. Furthermore the breakdown of the Tripartite Conference was followed by the most grave anti-Greek riots in Istanbul and Smyrna. These riots, which were instigated by the Turkish government, were of the most bloody and disgusting kind, recalling the days of Abdul Hamid. The purpose behind these riots was to drive a wedge between the Turkish community in Cyprus and the Greek majority and to serve notice on the Greek government that any appeal to the United Nations could be futile in the face of such accumulated Turkish fury. Indeed, the United Nations General Assembly on 23rd September, 1955, voted against the Greek request to place the question of Cyprus on the agenda. This failure left the Archbishop powerless to resist the intensification of violence throughout the island as his policy of relying on the United Nations was obviously not bearing fruit. The violence, in turn, obliged the British government to declare a state of emergency in Cyprus (a sign of political defeat) and to appoint Field Marshal Sir John Harding both as Governor and Commander-in-Chief in Cyprus. This was the net result of the five-year struggle against the tide of *enosis*.

Field Marshal Harding began his new regime in Cyprus by banning the left-wing group A.K.E.L.[5] and arresting 135 of its members. It is a matter of common knowledge, however, that A.K.E.L. declared itself against the armed struggle, a fact brought up against them by Colonel Grivas.

With the appointment of Field Marshal Harding the British government changed its tactics and for the first time encouraged direct negotiations between the Archbishop and the Governor. The meetings were held in a cordial atmosphere and Harding extended to the Archbishop the possibility of recognizing the principle of self-determination, which in itself marked a retreat from Macmillan's statement at the Tripartite Conference. Makarios insisted throughout on the principle of self-determination being recognized by the British government as a prior condition, thus showing that he knew when to modify his attitude towards *enosis*. However, on 20th October the talks broke down due to the fact that Makarios rejected the participation of both the Greek and Turkish governments in talks on any future Constitutions for the island. The rejection of Greece seems surprising, but the admission that Greece had a right to formulate the future Constitution of Cyprus after self-determination would have meant that Turkey could not be excluded as well. All the time the Archbishop had to guard against persistent attempts on the part of the British government to draw Turkey into the Cyprus dispute, which could partly have been to avoid alienating Turkey as an ally.

Despite these manœuvres the negotiations continued and Makarios was obviously making progress with Harding. As a matter of fact the Archbishop was making such progress in his talks with the Governor that the government in London thought that Harding was not capable of dealing with the astute Cypriot leader. The idea of a blunt soldier engaged in delicate negotiations with the prince of the Church seemed somewhat far-fetched and too much to the soldier's disadvantage. On 26th February, 1956, Lennox-Boyd, the then Colonial Secretary, flew to Cyprus to settle the question of self-determination. It is possible that Lennox-Boyd had been sent to Cyprus to torpedo the Makarios-Harding dialogue. He adopted a very truculent attitude towards the Archbishop. It seems that both Eden and Boyd became convinced that the great concessions which Makarios was willing to make, e.g. the shelving of *enosis*, were only a mask to be immediately followed by new demands. Their interpretation was that Makarios was willing to bury *enosis* in order to have self-determination but he would use self-determination once he got it, to destroy British influence for ever. Makarios was further hampered in the negotiations by events in Greece and the Arab world. Field Marshal Papagos had died and Greece had a new Prime Minister, Karamanlis, who adopted an attitude of extreme caution and did not back up Makarios at the crucial moment. The British had also just lost the Suez Canal base by making concessions to the Egyptians and were running into serious difficulties in Jordan, where early in March, 1956, as a result of a prolonged crisis, the young King dismissed the British Pro-consul General Sir John Glubb. It is obvious that Eden and his government felt shaken by the events in the Middle East and were now in no mood to contemplate any settlement in Cyprus. They wanted an excuse to get rid of Makarios in order, in his absence, to try for a solution in their favour. There is also the possibility that Makarios in 1956 held out too long, hoping for support from Greece, whereas in fact he was engulfed by the rising tide of troubles caused by the anti-Nasser struggle.

The result was that after one disastrous meeting with Lennox-Boyd the talks broke down and twelve days later Makarios and the Bishop of Kyrenia were seized by the British authorities and flown out to East Africa and then to the Seychelles Islands in the Indian Ocean.

It is paradoxical to contemplate the exile of Archbishop Makarios at the very moment when he was willing to compromise on the issue of *enosis* and *enosis* only. His political course ever since 1950 had been absolutely clear. He had consistently campaigned on the issue of *enosis* and thus, having gained immense popularity and established his political standing, could now afford to manœuvre. Self-determination could be used to exclude the Turkish danger brought out in the Cyprus situation by the British government. At the same time self-determination could provide himself and the Greek government with a breathing space. He could also claim that once self-determination had become an established fact anyone with any political acumen could bring about a situation whereby union with Greece could be effected, as happened formerly in the case of Crete. This would be possible if there were no provisions in the Constitution of Cyprus to prevent such a union taking place. Therefore, his policy must be such as to secure such a state of affairs and such a Constitution. As the evidence clearly shows, Makarios was always prepared to shelve the issue of *enosis* when it came to hard political bargaining. For this he has never been forgiven by the hardcore right-wingers within E.O.K.A. The British also moved against him for the opposite reasons, namely that he remained a partisan of *enosis* using the concept of self-determination as a clever trick to obscure his real motives. For this reason Eden and his advisers decided to get rid of him and they followed this up by an accusation that the Archbishop had personally actively organized terrorism in order to promote his political ends, whereas in fact the main intensification of violence came after he was no longer there to moderate it and to make the necessary compromises. The lesson had to be learned the hard way that, whether *enosis* or self-determination, these issues in Cyprus would have to be negotiated with the Archbishop, the only leader astute enough to maintain a balance between internal Cypriot division and the external contending powers.

X
The Return of Makarios

On 9th March, 1956, Makarios was removed from Cyprus for the time being. 'Removed' is the right word to use in the circumstances because the way in which the British authorities had organized the exile of the Archbishop lacked all the drama which one expects to be associated with such words as 'exile' and 'deportation'. There were no court proceedings or arrests; no dramatic gestures or riots, and certainly no imprisonment or even seizure of the Archbishop's person. Makarios was simply removed from Cyprus in a very ingenious way.

The Archbishop, after the ending of the negotiations between himself, Harding and Lennox-Boyd, was planning to go to Athens in order to consult the Greek government. And it must be realized here that a particular strangeness is associated with British policy over Cyprus, either due to British or Greek traditions or both. Imagine any other country having a rebellious province or colony which wanted to separate or to join another country, allowing the chief notary of that territory not only complete political freedom but every opportunity to travel freely in order to consult the government of the country which that territory wished to join, and which, morally at least, was supporting political upheaval in the subject territory. Imagine the French government of the Fourth Republic, during the

Algerian revolt, which raged at the same time as the crisis in Cyprus, allowing the chief Moslem notable in the country, wholly identified with the cause of Algerian independence, not only freedom and the power to negotiate but the opportunity to travel freely to consult, say, President Nasser in Cairo. Whatever the cause and the outcome of the Cyprus struggle, it must be admitted that on a comparative basis the British government had played the game according to the rules and, whatever the tone of the popular press, it went out of its way not to alienate the Hellenic spirit and to apply to the problem of Cyprus the new international morality stemming from the establishment of the United Nations. It can be said that Britain, wishing to maintain her colonial predominance in Cyprus adopted a policy which could only be described as anti-colonialist, given the behaviour of other countries in similar circumstances.

What happened on 9th March, 1956, was simply that Makarios and his travelling companions instead of being allowed to board the plane for Athens at Nicosia airport were told by the British authorities that they were being deported there and then, put on an R.A.F. transport plane, and flown out of Cyprus to an unknown destination. Actually the Archbishop knew what was going to happen before leaving his palace, and was quite prepared for what took place at the airport. Hardly any disturbances took place in Cyprus at his departure but the Greek government withdrew her ambassador from London.

The plane flew south and, out of the window, the exiles could see that they were over the Suez Canal area. They landed at Aden to refuel but were kept all the time on the plane. They then took off again and flew in the dark to land at dawn at Mombasa in Kenya. At the airstrip they were put on a bus and taken to comfortable quarters. But this was not the end of the journey.

After refreshments they were taken by car to the harbour and went by launch to a warship, which made off but remained outside the harbour for the night. At sea they were transferred to another warship H.M.S. *Loch Fada*. The warship headed east into the Indian Ocean. The Archbishop, a good historian and geographer, guessed their destination. He simply asked one of the officers: 'How long will it take us to get to the Seychelles?'[1] The officer replied that it would take about three days. The Archbishop knew that the Seychelles Islands had been used by the British government as a place of exile, the last political exiles being the leaders of the Palestine Arabs in 1937. The exiles were assigned a place of residence, Sans Souci Lodge, the Governor's country residence on the slopes of the mountain range overlooking Victoria harbour. Over £500 was spent in a great hurry to make the house habitable for a long period and a new hot-water system was installed. The British government in Cyprus granted the following allowances to the exiles:

Archbishop Makarios	£150 per month
Bishop Kyprianos	£100 per month
Rev. Papastavros	£50 per month
Mr. P. Ioannides	£50 per month

The exiles refused to accept these personal allowances except for family remittances.

Makarios and his companions arrived at Sans Souci Lodge on 14th March, 1956, at 2.30 p.m. Both bishops were dressed in their priestly robes, were wearing the medallions and chains of their office and carried long ivory-headed staffs. The appearance of Archbishop Makarios was particularly dignified, with deep-set dark eyes, most enigmatic, full of intelligence. The warrant of detention was not read at the Archbishop's request and instead an official letter was presented to the Archbishop informing him that he had open freedom of the Lodge and its grounds (approximately five acres), but was not allowed to go outside or to communicate with anyone without an official escort. There was no barbed wire around the Lodge, only a simple wire fence. Then tea was served.

During the next few days the party from Cyprus made themselves at home at the Lodge. The Archbishop changed his bedroom because it was next to that of the Bishop of Kyrenia whose snores kept him awake at night.

From the Lodge there was a magnificent view of Victoria harbour, 800 feet below, and the sea and islands near Mahe. The road to the Lodge from Victoria is extremely precipitous and serves to isolate it, which recommended it for security reasons. These security purposes were served by a police guard housed in the Lodge garage and a battery of powerful lights which were considered necessary as a precaution against any attempt of rescue by commandos landed by submarine. The servants' quarters were 25 yards from the guardroom. They and a guard of two N.C.O.s and six men, all unarmed, completed the entourage of the Archbishop and his fellow exiles. The internees and their residence, the servants, and the guards were under the supervision of Captain P. S. Le Geyt, late of the Indian Army and the Uganda Police, who had retired to the Seychelles for reasons of health, and whose account of the Archbishop and his party during their stay under his care is the principal source of information on the deportment of the Archbishop during his period of enforced exile.

However, the internees were still prisoners. The authorities feared that they would be rescued by a landing party either from a submarine or coming by air, or that Greek sailors from one of the many Greek ships in the Indian Ocean might try to rescue the Archbishop. Better fences were proposed and police dogs were imported from Kenya to patrol round the perimeter of the Lodge. This caused friction between the internees and the authorities, resulting in a hunger strike. This difficulty was only cleared up in June when the internees gave their parole to the government of the island not to try to escape. A little difficulty was caused here by the fact that, being priests, they took the meaning of parole literally and maintained that their word was enough. They would not sign any documents with their names, and the impasse was only resolved by the happy compromise of initialling the document. The parole gave the internees the freedom of the island and its capital, Victoria. They could, on informing the authorities, leave Sans Souci Lodge for picnics and trips round the island and for shopping expeditions at Victoria. However, they still could not communicate with unauthorized persons and it was suggested to them that they should always go about with an escort. The purpose of the escort was not so much to guard the Archbishop and his companions but to act as a guide and interpreter and to protect them in case of any incidents, as there was a certain amount of hostility from the British element, on political grounds, to the Archbishop on the island.

The Archbishop and his companions went on picnics all over the island, swam in the sea and the Archbishop insisted on climbing the high peaks on the island of Mahe. Shopping was done in Victoria, where the Archbishop bought a very large stuffed turtle. Apart from this, friendly relations were established with both the Roman Catholic and Anglican clergy on the island. On the whole the Archbishop arranged his day in the following way, according to Captain Le Geyt:

He was an early riser—6 a.m. At 6.30 a.m. he washed and dressed and had a walk in the grounds until 8 a.m. when he had breakfast. He would then sit under a mango tree and read his bible and meditate until 10.30 a.m. when he would read the papers, or a book, until 11 a.m.; he retired to his room, or his tent, to write or study until lunch at 1 p.m. He would rest between 2 and 3 p.m. and then study, or have his English lesson until about 5.30 p.m. The evening walk in the company of the Rev. Papastavros and Mr. Ioannides, or sometimes alone, would follow. They returned at about 6.30 p.m. and then they all met and talked on the verandah until 7.30 p.m. dinner. At 8 p.m. Radio Seychelles relayed the B.B.C. news from London, and then further conversation took place on the verandah until 10 p.m. when they all gathered round the wireless to hear the news in Greek from Athens. And so to bed, by 11 p.m.

The English lessons mentioned were given to the Archbishop by Mr. Stanley Jones, a retired district commissioner from Tanganyika, a person described by Captain Le Geyt as one of the 'Old School'. However, after the revelation of the *Grivas Diaries* in September 1956, Mr. Jones declined to continue his lessons with the Archbishop. His place was ultimately taken by Mrs. Margaret Le Geyt, wife of the amiable Captain Le Geyt. Mrs. Le Geyt recollects that it was a double pleasure to her to assist the Archbishop in his studies, both because of the intellectual quality of his mind and because of the stories which he recounted to her during the course of his lessons. In the end she admits that she learned more from the Archbishop than he from her.

The Archbishop, when at Sans Souci, did not wear his robes, but an open-necked dark blue shirt and black trousers which made him look much younger, and less majestic. His interest in and feeling for the English language were extraordinary in their sensitivity. Indeed, at a subsequent date he was attacked by his political opponents for studying the language of the 'enemy' during his exile. Mrs. Le Geyt recalls that for reading practice he chose articles from magazines on psychology and history and on one occasion the whole lesson was devoted to *British Table Manners*. Very quickly the Archbishop arranged in his imagination a table for a large dinner party. He explained his meticulous interest in table etiquette for which he is famous.[2]

But most of his lessons which the Archbishop had with Mrs. Le Geyt consisted of his extremely interesting reminiscences of his youth and previous career. He told her of his early days at Kykko monastery, and of his initiation. Mrs. Le Geyt had visited Kykko on a holiday from Egypt, and remembered seeing schoolboys at play there. One of them, aged about fourteen, was the Archbishop. He then went on to tell her about his student days in Athens, before and during the war, and mentioned that his favourite among the art treasures of Athens was the 'Sleeper' by Halepas. He then disclosed to her that his studies had developed in him a great admiration for Origen, despite the fact that he was later denounced as a heretic because his teaching was, on certain subjects, contrary to that of the official Church.

This is very indicative of the Archbishop's independence of mind in all matters, religion included.

The Archbishop then went on to talk about his episcopal duties. He told her that ever since his consecration he had paid the utmost attention to oratory and the art of the sermon. He admitted that he prepared his speeches extremely carefully, working very hard and learning them by heart. His speeches and sermons are never extemporary despite their fluency.

8 Meeting with General Grivas in Rhodes, 1959, after termination
of E.O.K.A. activities

9 The Non-aligned Conference in Belgrade, 1961

10 Makarios's visit to Turkey, 1962, talking at Ankara Airport with General Gürsel, President of the Republic of Turkey

11 Makarios with the late President Kennedy, on his State visit to Washington, January 1962

The main difficulty connected with the Archbishop's studies of English was the fact that in a small island like the Seychelles the amount of literature was limited. The Archbishop read *The Five Hundred Best Letters in the English Language*, which were travellers' talks of the 18th and 19th centuries—the Archbishop expressed admiration for Oscar Wilde's *De Profundis*. They also read together the play by Jane Bridie, *Tobias and the Angel*, in which the Archbishop took the part of both the Archangel and Satan. The Archbishop declared that in Greek his favourites were the great tragedians—because their plays treat of human fate and lead through pathos to catharsis.

During the course of these pleasant lessons the Archbishop admitted that his exile was perhaps a welcomed break from his labours, giving him an opportunity for reading, studying and writing his memoirs. Previously he had very little time for such activities in Cyprus, being constantly besieged by people. Once, he recalled, in order to get some peace he told his butler at nine o'clock to tell his callers anything he liked in order that he should not be troubled. At about 12.30 p.m. he heard angry voices saying that the Archbishop could not be still in his bath. Apparently his butler had told his callers that he was having a bath and continued to repeat the same story when they returned.

One of the negative aspects of the Archbishop's exile was that no one could communicate with him and his companions without all matter being first passed through the Cyprus government. Letters and communications addressed directly to the exiles in the Seychelles had to be returned to Cyprus for censorship, which delayed matters considerably. Censorship was also applied to all communications directed by the deportees to Cyprus, and the Archbishop had several of his letters returned to

H

him as unsuitable. The other was the publication by the British government in Cyprus in September 1956 of the notorious *Grivas Diaries* which made out that Makarios was personally the leader and instigator of the campaign of violence and the organiser of cold-blooded killings. This accusation was a great blow to the Archbishop and according to eyewitnesses induced a great feeling of despondency in the exiles. This was natural, as it was aimed at undermining the Archbishop's bargaining position by attacking his morals, quite apart from his political standing. Yet hardly had the ink dried which had been poured out over the *Grivas Diaries* when the Suez adventure undermined the whole British position in the Middle East. The unsavoury moral aspect of the British participation in the attack on Egypt made it very difficult for the British government and its successor to preach morality to anybody else. After the fall of the Eden government the new administration under Harold Macmillan resolved to take positive steps, as far as possible, to achieve some kind of settlement acceptable to all parties concerned. This new course was encouraged, no doubt, by great successes of E.O.K.A. which were scored due to the slackening of military measures in Cyprus as a result of Suez.

Even before the fall of Eden the British government had produced the so-called Radcliffe Constitution— a relatively liberal proposal for the solution of the Cyprus problem, although for the time being it excluded *enosis*. The Radcliffe proposals were rejected by Greece, and in Cyprus, in the absence of the Archbishop, nobody was available to negotiate on these proposals. The climax came when Greece again took the case of Cyprus to the United Nations and this time, in the atmosphere of Suez, an Indian resolution was adopted by the Political Committee placing the issue of Cyprus on the agenda.

The British government decided to release the Archbishop from exile if he would give an undertaking to make a 'clear appeal' to end violence in Cyprus. On 28th February, 1957, Makarios published a letter in the Seychelles asking E.O.K.A. to suspend all operations but, at the same time, making this dependent on the British government abolishing the state of emergency in Cyprus and declaring a certain amnesty. On 28th March, 1957, the Archbishop gave a press conference and declared that he was not prepared to negotiate about Cyprus unless he were permitted to return home. On the same day Mr. Lennox-Boyd told the House of Commons that it was no longer necessary to continue the Archbishop's detention, though he would not be allowed to return to Cyprus.

Before the Archbishop left the tropical island which had been the place of his exile for over a year, he arranged to make a gift of £1,000 to the island for the purpose of establishing a scholarship for the education of a boy and a girl in the Seychelles. Then followed receptions and parties for the Advisory Committee which the Archbishop organized to administer his gift, for various ecclesiastical and education representatives who had visited him, and for persons with whom he had come in contact officially. Indeed, the last week of the Archbishop's stay in the Seychelles was one continuous party. On 4th April the Archbishop held his official reception at which the Roman Catholic and Anglican clergy were present, and also Mr. Stanley Jones who had refused to teach the Archbishop English. The last festivity of all was a party for the Sans Souci Lodge servants and their families. They were served and entertained by the Archbishop and his companions in the true Christian spirit.

The next day, 6th April, 1957, the Archbishop and his

party left the island of their exile on board the tanker *Olympic Thunderer* sent by Mr. Aristotle Onassis to pick up the Archbishop and his companions and carry them to Madagascar from whence they proceeded to Athens.

Before leaving the island the Archbishop communicated the following sentiments to the editor of *Le Seychelles*:

'I have visited many places all over the world and it is no exaggeration to say that the Seychelles Islands contain the most beautiful places I have ever seen.

'I don't like to question Gordon's belief that the Seychelles were the Biblical Garden of Eden, but it is certainly a place which is entitled by its very nature to have this name. If these islands were nearer to the continent thousands of tourists would be their visitors. But perhaps the location willed that they should be isolated so that the primitive natural beauty He created should not be destroyed. To my eyes the loveliness became even more enhanced on the day that I became free.

'I had hoped to have a few days before leaving in which to visit other places here that I have not yet seen. But a Greek ship, the *Olympic Thunderer*, is calling for us tonight and as I have only just returned from a hurried one-day visit to Praslin— I must now say "Farewell" to the Seychelles.

'Before leaving I want to say, on behalf of my colleagues and myself, how grateful we are for the kindness and consideration with which we have been treated here by all those with whom we came in contact, and by the people employed in the Sans Souci household.

'So, when our ship leaves harbour, we shall take with us many good and kindly memories of the

Seychelles, and we wish the people of these islands happiness and prosperity.

'May God bless them all.'[3]

Archbishop Makarios

Sans Souci,
April 5th, 1957.

The Archbishop arrived in Athens from his exile on 17th April, and received a hero's welcome from the people. From now on, near his beloved native island and yet removed from it, he had to face the whirlpool of international politics. The return of the Archbishop was the turning point and it became obvious to all concerned that no progress could be made in strife-torn Cyprus as long as he could not return in triumph to his homeland.

PART D

XI
The years of E.O.K.A.

There is a well-known dictum of Spinoza which says that the contemplation of political passions moves sensible people to laugh, to weep, and to groan in that order.[1]

This comes painfully to mind when contemplating the whole history of the Cyprus problem as it developed in the 1950's. What was the purpose of it? Could the British governments at that period advance a solution without the useless bloodshed and the loss of so many British, Greek and Turkish lives? The answer must be no.

The exile of Makarios solved nothing. It did not bring as a result any of the advantages which some people in Britain hoped would flow from it. It seems that the decision to remove Makarios from Cyprus at this juncture was prompted by the hope that in his absence new, more pliable leaders would emerge and that the E.O.K.A. campaign would falter. Nothing of the kind happened. The result was the exact opposite. Makarios in exile in the Indian Ocean became a martyr for his own people and an international hero. Nothing, but absolutely nothing, could have placed the Archbishop on such an indestructible pedestal as the sole and undisputed leader of the Cypriots as his exile. There was no question of anybody else moving forward, and one begins to wonder if the object of his exile had not been exactly this, namely to strengthen and build up the Archbishop as against the E.O.K.A. leadership. The Archbishop's removal from Cyprus did not lead to the decline of E.O.K.A. but, on the contrary, the period from 1956 to the end of 1958 can be described in truth as the years of E.O.K.A.

The part played by the Governor, Field Marshal Sir John Harding, in the deportation of the Archbishop, which smacked of deception, did not go unrewarded: soon afterwards he had the distinction of sleeping soundly through the night with an E.O.K.A. time-bomb under his mattress. Charles Foley, the most reliable eyewitness of events in Cyprus, summed up the situation in the island after the deportation of the Archbishop in one terse sentence: 'E.O.K.A. was attacking with fresh vigour all over the island.'[2] Actually it was about this time that the British authorities in Cyprus finally realized that their opponent, 'Dighenis', was Colonel George Grivas, a retired regular officer in the Greek Army, and not Archbishop Makarios in person. The result of the whole rigmarole was that the Archbishop's deportation produced the inevitable political void in which nothing could be accomplished and nothing was accomplished. Moreover, and this should have been realised by those responsible, the Archbishop's physical presence in Cyprus had been a moderating and restraining influence: up to the time of his exile the E.O.K.A. campaign, with some exceptions, had consisted of sabotage, stoning and scuffles; after the departure of the Archbishop the situation deteriorated rapidly. For example, acts of violence in March 1956, were 246, the highest monthly total so far; there were 234 incidents in April, 295 in May, and 276 in June.[3]

May 1956 also saw the first two executions of young Cypriots, Karaolis and Demetriou, convicted of E.O.K.A.

activities, which brought passions in Cyprus to a high
pitch. After these events there was an escalation of both
E.O.K.A. activities and military activities directed by
Harding against it until August, 1956, when Colonel
Grivas suggested a truce prompted by the changing
political situation in the eastern Mediterranean. However, the truce did not last long, being shattered by a
bomb explosion on August 25th which resulted in the
most intense period of attacks on the British garrison in
Cyprus and the Cyprus authorities during the whole of
the emergency period.

The autumn of 1956 was a crucial period for everybody
concerned in the Cyprus problem. Britain was about to
embark on her ill-advised Greek adventure and in the
Seychelles Makarios was gravely embarrassed by the
publication in September of the so-called *Grivas Diaries*.
These 'Diaries' were part of the papers of Colonel
Grivas sold to the British authorities by a Cypriot who
had been charged with looking after a part of the
E.O.K.A. secret archives. The truth of the matter can
never be established, as Colonel Grivas has always
been a voluminous writer and a compulsive diarist. The
amount of the thoughts of Colonel Grivas handed over
to the authorities was imposing, and with such material
in hand it was easy to produce selected passages, quoted
out of context, to show that Makarios was the actual
leader of a bloody campaign of violence whereas, in
fact, as Grivas had recorded in his genuine *Memoirs*,[4]
not always friendly to Makarios, the Archbishop had
always exercised a restraining and impeding influence, wanted the campaign to be restricted to
sabotage, and had only accepted Grivas's organization
when it was forced on him by the pressure of events.[5]
For instance, Grivas, a trained soldier, made the point
over and over again that the Archbishop remained

blind to the guerrilla warfare. Makarios also emphatically vetoed, after his release from exile in March 1957, the scheme put forward by Grivas to set up an E.O.K.A. execution team in London, where many Cypriot traitors had taken refuge. Anyhow, the affair of the *Grivas Diaries* was used by the British government to justify the deportation of Makarios and to veto his return to Cyprus in any capacity until conditions had been created which made it unlikely that he would become a serious danger to security. The British government, then under Anthony Eden, agreed with Harding that there could be no new move concerning the Archbishop unless he were to denounce the use of violence. 'Denouncing terrorism' soon became a formula from which Governor Harding and the government in London could not escape. However, as Foley remarks: 'But for Makarios to denounce terrorism meant to repudiate men who had become national heroes; and for long this impossible condition was made a requisite to political progress.'[6]

The true climax of the Cyprus problem came, as already mentioned, at the end of 1956. The Suez adventure can now be seen in retrospect to have been the beginning of the end, and the only complaint is that the end was unnecessarily delayed. The Suez adventure cost Britain her position in the Middle East and with its loss the whole relationship between Britain and Cyprus altered. There had been a war and it was followed by neither peace nor honour. During the fighting on the Canal, Cyprus had served as a base for this exploit. 'The roads were crowded with stores and personnel—ideal targets for guerrillas.'[7]

During November, 1956, E.O.K.A. made 416 attacks, the highest monthly figure ever, in which over 40 people, mostly soldiers, were killed. There was also a full-scale attack on bases and equipment. Numerous vehicles and aeroplanes were destroyed; military stores were fired; and there was widespread sabotage against all military installations. Bombers were destroyed at the air base of Akrotiri and the military cantonments at Episkopi and Deghelia were thoroughly bombed. If Cyprus were to be a base for British military operations in the Middle East then, as the events of November, 1956, proved, it would itself no longer be safe from war. One wonders if Britain would have suffered so much in Cyprus during that fatal month had Archbishop Makarios been functioning at the Archbishopric instead of going on picnics in the Seychelles.

The Suez affair also resulted in the elimination of Eden as well as other diehards from the British government. The new Prime Minister, Harold Macmillan, was unlikely to make the same mistakes as his predecessors. One of the first acts was to terminate the Archbishop's exile, though not resuming political contact with him, which was in the circumstances a tragic mistake. Another move towards ending bloodshed in Cyprus by the Macmillan government was the offer of the so-called Radcliffe Constitution, though here, to be fair, Lord Radcliffe had been asked to frame his constitutional solution for Cyprus by Eden when he was still Prime Minister.

This is no place to examine the legal niceties of the Radcliffe Constitution. It will be sufficient to examine its two most prominent features: (1) The idea of *enosis* was dropped in favour of complete independence and sovereignty. (However, it is true that *enosis* was not ruled out for the remote future.) (2) The Radcliffe proposals were based on Cyprus enjoying majority rule, and there was no question of any partition or sovereign Turkish areas. The proposed Constitution was at once rejected by Greece, even before any Cypriots (including Archbishop

Makarios) had seen it, on the ground that it did not guarantee self-determination at any given date and because the Governor's veto was held to deny self-government. Makarios, when informed of the constitutional proposals in the Seychelles, rejected them as well, on the grounds that he could not consider any constitutional proposals while in exile and because the proposed Constitution seemed to be aimed at the continuation of colonialism, and because it had been previously rejected by Greece. At this time Makarios was still pinning his hopes on the United Nations where another Greek resolution was coming up asking the Assembly to set up a fact-finding committee to investigate the charges and counter-charges of terrorism in Cyprus. The result was an Indian resolution which expressed hope for an atmosphere of peace and freedom in Cyprus and led to Grivas calling another truce to come into operation 'as soon as the Archbishop is released'.

The release of the Archbishop was made conditional on the old formula of 'denouncing terrorism' and this was demanded in a statement made in the House of Commons on 20th March, 1957, by Lennox-Boyd. Makarios published his reply on 28th and did not include a 'clear appeal' to end violence in Cyprus. He simply asked E.O.K.A. 'to declare cessation of all operations, given that the British Government will show a spirit of understanding by abolishing simultaneously the present state of emergency . . .' He thus repeated a passage from a letter he had written to Harding on 2nd February, 1956, in which he made a condition of agreement that emergency military measures and emergency legislation should be revoked and an amnesty for all political offences granted. The Archbishop also referred to the United Nations resolution calling for a peaceful, democratic and just solution of the problem and stressed that it was a starting point towards a settlement of the issue. He mentioned that he understood this resolution as 'an expression of the wish of the United Nations for bilateral negotiations between the British Government and the people of Cyprus'. He ended his letter by expressing that it was in the spirit of this United Nations resolution, and in order to facilitate a resumption of such negotiations, that E.O.K.A. was willing to call a truce if he were released.[8]

Makarios arrived in Athens from his exile on April 17th, 1957, and received a hero's welcome. He took up his headquarters in a suburban villa and installed the polished shell of a giant Seychelles turtle in his study to remind him of the need for patience. He wrote to Macmillan preparing the resumption of talks where they had been broken off by his 'kidnapping' but Macmillan refused. His main concerns at this time were the stories of alleged atrocities committed against not only E.O.K.A. suspects but also civilians by British troops. On one occasion he showed a visitor 317 statements concerning ill-treatment by British troops.[9] He then departed for a visit to the United States.[10] At this stage Makarios refused to accept mediation by N.A.T.O. but he favoured 'a temporary solution' of placing the island under U.S. mandate. It is of significance that in his letter to Macmillan he mentioned 'freedom for Cyprus' rather than union with Greece. This shift of emphasis from union to freedom and independence in itself went a long way to solve the objections being raised by the Turkish minority and the Turkish government, though he consistently resisted the right of the Turks to take an equal part in any negotiations on the future of Cyprus, in which he was supported by the Greek government. In the meantime the Turkish underground movement V.O.L.C.A.N. was crossing swords with E.O.K.A., as the Turkish minority, inspired from Ankara, began demanding the partition of Cyprus. It is interesting to note that the Turkish government shifted from opposing the union of Cyprus with Greece to demanding the partition of the island or even the return of Cyprus to Turkey.

Sir John Harding, after two years of service in Cyprus, left in October, 1957. He had failed to defeat Colonel George Grivas and E.O.K.A., and opposed the return of Makarios to Cyprus on the grounds that Makarios was a 'threat to security'. In his opinion nothing would be more disastrous than to allow the return of the Archbishop.[11] Little did he realize that by removing Makarios and failing to crush Grivas he had thrust political responsibility on the E.O.K.A. leader, with results that could well have been avoided had the Archbishop been there. Although Harding was succeeded by a governor of very different stamp, Sir Hugh Foot, the fact remained that, during the period of change-over between governors and because Sir Hugh Foot was a civilian, security and policy in respect of E.O.K.A. fell entirely into the hands of the Army. The Governor made every effort at this stage to win the confidence of the Turkish minority as well and because the course of events had destroyed confidence there was an escalation of violence and bitterness.

Grivas was growing disappointed with both the Greek government and Makarios, and in March, 1958, he launched a new campaign of passive resistance and economic boycott of British goods. This proved very unpopular among the business community who, in turn, naturally turned to the Archbishop, who took their side. He immediately wrote to Grivas ordering him to show more flexibility. Grivas gave vent to his accumulating bitterness against Makarios by writing:

12 Official visit of Makarios to India, 1962

13 Welcome at Berlin Airport by Willy Brandt, on State visit, May 1962

14 Visit to Egypt, 1961

15 The British Prime Minister, Harold Wilson, accompanied by his wife, greets the Archbishop on the occasion of a dinner for Commonwealth Leaders

'I am amazed at the unscrupulous way in which the Archbishop has tried to convey his views. He has never sent any instructions about the boycott, yet now he tries to interfere and upset everything . . .'[12]

Evidence that the political situation in Cyprus, in the continued absence of Makarios, was placing Grivas in a position of political authority came to the fore when Sir Hugh Foot requested a secret meeting with him. Grivas suspected a trick and, indeed, it cannot be ruled out that the authorities may have been attempting to split the leadership of the Cypriots.

In the continued absence of the Archbishop violence could not be stamped out. Suspicions lingered, informers were at work and the military continued the ill-treatment of internees. E.O.K.A. replied with guns and Sir Hugh Foot was forced to bring back the emergency regulations first promulgated by Harding which, among other things, made the death penalty mandatory for carrying arms. Sir Hugh Foot departed for London in May 1958 in order to urge the government to elaborate a new solution to the Cyprus problem. Grivas responded by calling a truce until further notice.

The new British plan of June, 1958, amounted in practice to a triple condominium in which Britain would share the island with Greece and Turkey, and it was rejected both by the Greek and Turkish governments. The Archbishop described the plan as something that was wholly unacceptable and ran counter to the fundamental and alienable right of the people of Cyprus to self-determination.[13] This was the famous Macmillan Plan and it did nothing to abate violence in Cyprus. The British were now paying dearly for the absence of the Archbishop from the island, and Macmillan was beginning to realize at last that there could be no settlement in Cyprus without the Archbishop, who was the sole

I

spokesman for the Greek community. Macmillan introduced some modifications to his plan, including some
form of representative institutions, which were lacking
in the original. Makarios obviously now had the upper
hand and wrote to the Governor telling him that he could
not entertain the new plan, as the people of Cyprus
could never accept a plan which disregarded their basic
democratic rights and denied them both freedom and
peace.

August, 1958, saw the final E.O.K.A. offensive against
the British troops in Cyprus. The attacks were deadly
and included the destruction of British bases and aircraft.
On 15th September E.O.K.A. announced it would strike
at British civilians in Cyprus. Certain members of the
British community in Cyprus were killed for their co-
operation with the colonial regime.

There is no denying that E.O.K.A. did its job and
forced the British government to revise its attitude towards the island as a whole; to return to negotiations
with Makarios; and to give up any attempt to impose
its own particular solution of the problem. On the other
hand, Makarios showed himself quite capable of seizing
the right moment to exercise his political gifts. In
September 1958 he made perhaps his most significant
political move up to date. He unequivocally shifted
emphasis from *enosis* to independence on the basis of
self-determination and self-government. This move
enabled the British, Greek and Turkish governments
to begin the uphill task of resolving the Cyprus tangle.
From here on the road lay to London via Zürich. As
Makarios desired the independence of Cyprus, and
independence within the British Commonwealth, neither
Greece nor Turkey was going to have Cyprus; British
honour was satisfied. E.O.K.A. suspended operations
on Christmas Eve, 1958, though the British Army

continued to comb the mountains and tried to track down the organization. The hour of Makarios was rapidly approaching as the Foreign Ministers of Greece and Turkey finally met in Zürich to shake hands and settle the question of Cyprus 'in the spirit of Atatürk and Venizelos'.

XII
Triumph and Compromise

Up to the end of 1958, E.O.K.A. was the only form of resistance offered to the British government in Cyprus. The task which Colonel Grivas allotted himself was to make Cyprus as unpleasant as possible for the British in order to prove that in such circumstances it could never provide a satisfactory base for Britain in the Middle East; and to disgrace the British government by exposing it to ridicule for being unable to capture him and to crush his organization. Politically, however, Grivas could not lead. The Archbishop, in his exile in Athens, was the only man who could change the political situation in Cyprus. He had to guard against many dangers. Contrary to the views promulgated by some organs of the British press he was not on good terms with the Greek government and his mounting fear, both as a politician and a Cypriot, was that the opportunist Greek government of Karamanlis would get together with Britain and Turkey to impose a solution on Cyprus which he believed would not be in the interest of the Cypriots themselves.

The danger was that the Macmillan government would press ahead with the imposition of its own solution on Cyprus. This solution implied a de facto partition of the island and the so-called Macmillan Plan, although based on 'partnership', authorized the setting up of separate Greek and Turkish municipal councils; politicians were using the time-honoured device of divide and rule. Makarios felt that he had to move quickly in order to prevent the destruction of his homeland—a matter not perhaps appreciated by the Greek government nor, indeed, by some of his lieutenants. It was on 7th September, 1958, that Makarios made his historic decision. He told the Greek government privately that he was now ready to accept independence for Cyprus after a period of self-government. He then used the occasion of an interview with Mrs. Barbara Castle, M.P. (then member of the Labour Executive), to announce his decision to the world. In other words, *enosis* and only *enosis*, the return of Cyprus to Greece, in the name of which the struggle was launched, was to be side-stepped for the sake of a broader settlement, bearing in mind the international situation. He knew now that the only hope for success at the United Nations lay in asking for self-determination. Otherwise the Greek Cypriots might be faced with a *fait accompli*. The imposition of the Macmillan Plan would lead to partition or would give the Turks (the Ankara government) an impregnable position in Cyprus. He had to move quickly and take the risk of being misunderstood or even branded as a traitor.

The Archbishop's decision burst like a bombshell on E.O.K.A. Grivas wrote in his *Memoirs*: 'His [the Archbishop's] failure to prepare the ground with the Cypriot public in advance also showed a dangerous lack of psychological understanding; I was forced to take immediate action to reassure the Organization.'[1] Makarios made his ideas on the situation clear in a letter to Grivas:

'As you will have read in the newspapers yester-day, I made a statement to Mrs. Barbara Castle, the M.P., by which I virtually created a new situ-

133

ation. I declared that if the British government abandoned the Macmillan-Foot plan, I would be willing, after a fixed period of self-government, to accept a regime of independence which would not be transformed except by decisions of the U.N. Although this new line could possibly be described as a retreat, it is what the situation, if coldly appraised, requires.

'My latest information is extremely disheartening. ... British public opinion has turned very considerably against us, and the British press, including that of the Labour party, even when not attacking us, carefully avoids any kind of publication which would damage the prestige of British troops, because of the strength of public opinion.

'Barbara Castle and others among the Labour party declared that they could not oppose the British plan unless the Archbishop offered something new which would be favourably received under the conditions at present prevailing in England. If this was done they said they would urge the Archbishop's views on the British Prime Minister and put them forward at the party conference and through their newspapers.

'I cannot now forecast the consequences, but they cannot be bad. America has completely aligned its policies with Britain and our only hope of success at the U.N. is to put the question on the basis of independence ...

'We had to face up to the situation realistically and reach a decision before we were presented with a *fait accompli*, for the imposition of the British plan, no matter how bold and determined the resistance of the Greek people in Cyprus, would inevitably lead to partition, or would give the Turks rights which it

would be impossible (even under different conditions) to remove later.'[2]

This letter was treated with an outburst of anger by
Colonel Grivas. Not being in Athens, Colonel Grivas
could not understand the crisis around the Archbishop
which is well evident in what Makarios told Sir Hugh
Foot when they met at the Hotel Grande Bretagne in
Athens, during Mr. Macmillan's visit there to promote
his plan for a Greek-Turkish condominium in Cyprus.
Makarios urged Foot to abandon the Macmillan Plan.
It might be better to propose an independent Cyprus
within the Commonwealth; it was unwise to propose
bringing in divided rule and viceroys from Greece and
Turkey. Sir Hugh Foot commented that the Archbishop
spoke as a Greek. To which Makarios replied: 'No, I
talk as a Cypriot. I ask that Greece, as well as Turkey,
should be left out of any decision on my country.'[3]

As it was, a solution was imposed on Cyprus which
was arrived at, in the absence of the Archbishop, at
Zürich in February, 1959, by the governments of Greece
and Turkey, then represented by Karamanlis and
Menderes. To be quite fair, the Cypriot Turks were also
left out of the Zürich talks. Karamanlis, when he came
back from the Zürich conference, conferred with Makarios
for over two hours and showed him the agreements
which had been reached. Makarios later told the Press
that he had congratulated and thanked Karamanlis for
his efforts. But in private he expressed his deep anxiety.
He did not expect agreement at the Zürich conference.
When it came he found it very difficult to make up his
mind because he had been overtaken by events. His only
hope was to effect some changes through discussions to
be held in London. The hour of trial arrived for the
Archbishop when the three Powers, Britain, Greece and

Turkey, invited him to attend a conference in London on 17th February, 1959, at Lancaster House in order to accept the agreement. It was like an invitation to a shotgun wedding, and it was fortunate that Makarios was a clergyman. Indeed, in the circumstances, he needed all the composure of his ecclesiastical background to face the coming trial of strength.

The events in London were scheduled to proceed at a galloping pace. Mr. Macmillan had to leave almost immediately for his memorable visit to the Soviet Union, and he wanted to settle the Cyprus problem first. Makarios had to leave for London almost at once and in a great hurry he summoned twenty-four advisers from Cyprus to meet him in London. The delegation, when it reached London, was lodged at the Park Lane Hotel, where they were joined the next day by Makarios. It was there that he had to outline the core of the Zürich Agreement to the delegation, which had known nothing about it up to that time. This extraordinary pressure which Makarios applied to his delegation was only a reflection of the pressure which was being applied to him. His attendance at Lancaster House was not for the purpose of discussing the Zürich Agreement on the basis of equality but only for his assent and signature. He was entirely isolated and yet, because of the danger of partition, he could not refuse to sign or play for time. In other words, the Lancaster House Conference on Cyprus was a typical *Diktat*. Makarios was simply told to sign on the dotted line or to face the consequences. When faced with such a situation Makarios replied, 'If you insist on my saying "Yes" or "No" tonight then the answer must be "No".'[4] During the night Karamanlis applied the final turn of the screw by telling Makarios that Greece was committed to the Zürich Agreement and would wash its hands of Cyprus if the Archbishop refused to sign. Heated discussions went on throughout the night; Karamanlis and his Foreign Minister threatened Makarios; and Karamanlis is also reported to have got Queen Frederika of Greece to influence the Archbishop via telephone from Athens. In the face of this Greek betrayal Makarios was forced to accept the Zürich Agreement *in toto*, without any modifications. In view of what transpired later, this turned out to be a tragic oversight, hard as he had fought to alter the nefarious consequences inherent in the Agreement.[5]

Six years later the Archbishop himself described what happened in London in the following words:

'In London, I tried to get some changes made but there was not enough time to study the Agreement. But at the very first reading I singled out thirteen points which I raised again in 1963. I tried hard and failed.

'Selwyn Lloyd said at the last meeting: "This is an Agreement, a text on which we three governments agree. You expressed your views, and expressed disagreement on certain points. We have heard your views and we do not agree with you. You have to take it or leave it. Don't try for any change." Zorlu said: "We don't agree with your views. We talked for a week and came to an agreement and we can't go back on it." I said: "I was under the impression that I had come to discuss a solution of the Cyprus question, and not to sign what you three governments had already agreed upon. You put me in a difficult situation when you say, Take it or leave it." The answer was: "We don't agree."

'When I realized that it was impossible for me to change their minds, I asked for further time to think it over. "The answer has to be 'Yes' or 'No'," said Lennox-Boyd. I said: "It can't be decided 'Yes' or 'No'." Lennox-Boyd said he had been invited to the Far East and that it was only one day before Mr. Macmillan's trip to Moscow. "You must answer by this afternoon." So I said: "If you want my answer now, my answer is 'No'."

'The meeting was adjourned and it was agreed that I should have to give an answer by 10.30 the next morning. They said that if the answer were "Yes", would I please contact the Foreign Office and the last meeting would be held at Prime Ministers' level in the afternoon to sign an agreement. If the answer is "No", then, they said, "we shall issue a communiqué saying that the Conference has failed". There was no choice for me. They told me: "If you refuse, you will be responsible for all the repercussions in Cyprus. The world has put its hopes on the success of the Conference, and you will be responsible for its failure."

'I was sure that, if I did not sign the Agreement, there might be partition. Cyprus would be divided as a colony and we would not be able to raise the question again. The less bad thing was to sign. The next morning I telephoned the Foreign Office.'[6]

At the moment of his enforced signature, followed by Mr. Macmillan's handshake, Makarios seemed to have achieved his purpose (not to mention his ambition). His purpose has always been the freedom of his homeland and, up to that point, its union with Greece. It was fully understood, when he signed the Zürich Agreement, that independence was going to be interpreted as the necessary first step to union with Greece in the future. For the present, at the cost of severe sacrifices, the threat of partition hanging over Cyprus had been removed.

At least the Cypriots could be master in their own home, and Makarios knew that when he returned to Cyprus he would return as its political leader. After a struggle lasting nine years (1950–9) he was returning to his people in triumph. But it was a triumph which he had purchased at the cost of compromises, which not only deferred union with Greece but also were fraught with grave consequences for the future. This was the reason why he had tried to discuss the Zürich proposals before committing himself, though in vain. It is not surprising that he had sought to have the Zürich Agreement amended if the situation which it created is examined impartially.

The Zürich Agreement, ratified in London at Lancaster House, created a situation in Cyprus of extreme complexity from the constitutional and international points of view. Greece and Turkey acquired certain vested constitutional rights in the new Republic. This situation placed Cyprus in a unique position among the countries of the British Commonwealth in so far as two countries outside the Commonwealth had acquired rights in it. These rights, which are to be found in the Treaties of Guarantee between Cyprus, Britain, Greece and Turkey, and the Treaty of Alliance between Cyprus, Greece and Turkey, gave both Greece and Turkey the right of military intervention in Cyprus in case of a breach of the provisions of the Treaties. As the Constitution of the Republic of Cyprus had been drawn up at Zürich, without the representatives of the people of Cyprus being consulted, and as this Constitution provided for certain entrenched rights of the Turkish community, danger could be clearly sensed on the horizon in case of a constitutional deadlock. It was just a matter of time. The crux of the matter was that the Turkish Vice-President of the Republic, representing the minority, had the same powers of veto under the Constitution as the President of the Republic representing the majority. Furthermore, the Constitution envisaged, in addition to other measures pertaining to the Turkish minority, the division of the five main towns of the island into separate Greek and Turkish municipalities with their own elected councils and with the provision that within four years the President and the Vice-President of the Republic should examine whether or not this system of separate municipalities should continue.

It had been a hard struggle and that Makarios had come out of it unscathed in his popularity was a triumph of its kind. In reality the London Conference was a defeat (for the present at least) of some of his cherished hopes. That the Archbishop put the best face he could on his defeat, if defeated he was, was a triumph in itself. On March 1st, 1959, he returned to Cyprus where he was received by a storm of enthusiasm; and he spoke of victory.

XIII
Makarios: President of Cyprus

Makarios returned to Cyprus on 1st March, 1959, from Athens, three years after his departure arranged by the British authorities. Two hundred thousand people turned out to greet him in the streets of Nicosia. The Cyprus Broadcasting Service commentator caused general astonishment by crying out: 'At last our hero the Ethnarch is back and we hope soon to welcome another hero, the legendary Dighenis, who fought for our freedom and the freedom of our children.'[1] Indeed, although the Archbishop was back in Cyprus, his presence seemed only to be required in order to answer questions about Grivas—his whereabouts and his future plans. Makarios, faced with such morbid curiosity on the part of the gentlemen of the Press, folded his arms and said: 'Much patience will be needed.' He was right because after his ordeal in London he had now to justify his policy to those who had been fighting and dying for *enosis* on the soil of Cyprus. Grivas had no doubts about the issues at stake and spoke out accordingly:

'Archbishop Makarios ended his exile on 1st March, 1959, but my bitterness over the agreement was such that E.O.K.A. took no part in his Nicosia reception: I did not even send a representative to bid him welcome in spite of Averoff's windy phrase in Parliament the day before that "the whole of Cyprus with heroic Dighenis at its head, is gathering as one man to hail Makarios, creator of the independent State". The crowds were big enough, but they were not acclaiming the Agreement, merely the return of the Ethnarch.'[2]

The above judgement can be interpreted as being the angry outburst of an outraged patriot or the spleen of frustrated ambition. Did it not look as if Makarios had agreed with alacrity to every point in the Zürich and London Agreements, particularly independence, which would confirm him in power and send Grivas back to Greece? The impression was that a brave but blunt soldier had been outmanœuvred by a suave Byzantine intriguer. Grivas had not even been kept informed about the Zürich and London negotiations. When he challenged Makarios with this, Makarios replied that events had moved too fast.

On March 17th, 1959, Makarios arranged a farewell function for Grivas at which a semblance of good cheer was maintained. Makarios moved among the guests in his robes and his silver-topped staff, in contrast to Grivas who wore his famous uniform of bandoliered jersey and breeches together with binoculars and a revolver, while on his head he had the beige beret with the words E.O.K.A. embroidered in blue. It was Grivas who began to preach to the representatives of the Cypriot press on the virtues of unity. Turning to left-wing writers he told them that his purpose had never been to combat communism but to teach the people to work together for unity. Makarios then interposed: 'and Christianity'. Grivas agreed and gave out as his farwell message the cause of 'unity and Christianity'.[3] The Archbishop's next engagement with E.O.K.A. was when, after the departure of Grivas, all E.O.K.A. men, both from the towns and the mountains, called on him in Nicosia and he shook each one of them by the hand. Nevertheless, there was a wry taste about the whole affair. Makarios was a politician; the fighting men had fought for '*enosis* and only *enosis*'. Now in the hour of his triumph the Archbishop was departing on an unknown course.

The name of Makarios has become so inextricably attached to Cyprus that from now on everything that transpired on the island has been associated with his name and been attributed to him. But it is forgotten that in reality his hands were tied by the Zürich and London Agreements in the drafting of which he had taken no part. He has never departed from his basic belief that the Cypriots have the right to choose freely the type of government they want and the status the island should have, whether independence or *enosis*. He had to accept the 1959 compromise because he could not do otherwise. Now back in Cyprus he had to deal with various extremists, Communists, nationalists and armed groups not under his direct control. He has not always been successful in this and the odds against him have been great. In his extremely delicate position he had to choose his words carefully which has earned him the description of 'Byzantine', epitome of duplicity and devious intrigue.

For the time being, however, it was holiday time in Cyprus. There was a rush of cocktail parties, and the Archbishop was seen more often in the drawing room than at the altar. The Greek and Turkish navies paid courtesy calls. Makarios, the Turkish leader Dr. Küchük, Sir Hugh Foot and General Darling attended a gala party on board Kemal Atatürk's former yacht to partake of raki and Bosphorus lobster. The Archbishop now took salutes from the British troops and on one occasion sent personal compliments to the commander of the

Black Watch guard for 'an excellent turnout'.[4]

In the meantime Makarios was doing his best to pare down the size of the sovereign British bases accorded to Britain under the Agreements, from 120 square miles to 99. At the same time a more fundamental piece of wrangling was going on between Greek and Turkish lawyers on the terms of the proposed Constitution. The difficulty here was that the Constitution had to embody the Agreements reached at Zürich and London which provided the Turkish minority with such privileges that, although partition was excluded, the Constitution could hardly be workable.

Once the Constitution had been drafted the way was clear for elections, particularly for the election of the President of the Republic as provided by the Constitution. Everybody assumed that Makarios would become President by acclaim. This did not happen. The extreme right wing of E.O.K.A., with or without Grivas's prompting, now regarded Makarios as traitor to *enosis*, while the Communists and other left-wingers arrived at the conclusion that they disliked the followers of Grivas less they than they did the Archbishop. The two wings combined to form what they called the Democratic Union. The candidate of the Democratic Union was 73-year-old John Clerides, Q.C., C.B.E., an ex-mayor of Nicosia and an ex-member of the Legislative Council. In the midst of an electoral campaign full of vituperation and bitterness, where last year's heroes were denounced as traitors and vice versa, the National Front backing Makarios produced a damning photograph of Clerides shaking Sir John Harding by the hand and forgetting, with sublime indifference, that the Archbishop had shaken Harding by the hand on many more occasions than Clerides.

Makarios himself played little overt part in the campaign. He made a preaching tour of the island, speaking only in the churches, but his path through the town was strewn with myrtle branches, and crowds fought and wept and shouted to kiss his hand. The Democratic Union complained of a campaign of 'violence, bribery, threats, scandalous behaviour, and use of the cult of personality' but on 13th December, 1959, Makarios obtained 67 per cent of the total votes cast[5] and became the first President of the independent Republic of Cyprus.

On 16th August, 1960, Cyprus became an independent Republic and the 99th Member of the United Nations and at the same time a member of the British Commonwealth. On the next day, the 17th August, 1960, Sir Hugh Foot, the last Governor, left Cyprus from Famagusta harbour. The Archbishop-President was there to bid him farewell. What his thoughts were when he watched the destroyer bearing the Governor out of sight is difficult to tell. The struggle had been hard fought but it was not over. There were still British Forces present in Cyprus and the constitutional problem created by the Zürich and London compromise could produce as great a struggle in the future as the struggle which had just been terminated by the former Governor's departure.

On the political level Makarios now became transformed from colonial enemy to Commonwealth friend and ally. There was a honeymoon of goodwill. He attended the Commonwealth Prime Ministers' Conference in London and was introduced to the Queen. The former internee in the Seychelles was welcomed by Cabinet Ministers in London, and in 1961 Queen Elizabeth II paid a brief visit to Cyprus. The official photograph of the happy event shows Her Majesty and His Beatitude wearing smiles so warm as to suggest that this was a moment for which both of them had long waited. Otherwise Makarios did not change his mode of life very much. He continues to live in the Archiepiscopal Palace inside the walls of old Nicosia and only uses the Presidential Palace (the former Governor's House) as an office.

There is no doubt that between 1959 and 1963 the Archbishop-President became the symbol of moderation in Cyprus. He had come to occupy a middle position between the right and left in Cypriot politics; he was the symbol of co-operation between the Greek and Turkish communities in Cyprus, as the signatory of the Zürich and London Agreements; he was the protagonist in bringing Cyprus into the British Commonwealth. His role was described as such by the British press before its change of heart at the end of 1963 when it forgot all that it had been saying about him. During those years Makarios was indeed soft-pedalling the cause of *enosis*. There could have been several reasons for it. Perhaps he had become convinced that a precipitate union with Greece would not serve the best interests of the people of Cyprus. Perhaps he had come to enjoy his part as Head of State too much to abdicate from it. Perhaps he saw the way to *enosis* fraught with dangers arising from the Zürich and London Agreements and had decided to relegate it from the field of practical politics to that of ultimate desiderata. Anyway, a current joke circulating among cynics in Nicosia declared that the Archbishop was quite willing to agree to *enosis*, but only on his death-bed. However, the constitutional and political problems —the heritage of the bitter years of strife—were in themselves a task which would have made people much more formidable than the Archbishop shrink from any hasty ventures. And in this context, it must be remembered, the Archbishop, being a churchman, was never and can never be a revolutionary leader.[6]

The reconciliation between Makarios and Grivas did not last long. Very soon Grivas was launching attacks on Makarios in an extremist right-wing newspaper in Athens called *Estia*. The attacks were of such a nature that some of the Archbishop's admirers (unknown to him) went to the offices of the newspaper in Athens and beat up the editor. In Cyprus, too, the same thing happened to the editor of the newspaper *Ethniki*, Mr. Antonis Pharmakides, who in addition to being beaten up was also kidnapped and was only released after the personal intervention of the Archbishop. This incident completed the split in the former E.O.K.A. ranks in Cyprus, a split which had actually occurred long before the end of the emergency.

Grivas demanded the dismissal of the Minister of the Interior and his Police Chief. He also declared that Makarios was not fit to govern, charging him with timidity, vacillation and trickery throughout the struggle; he accused him of plotting with the Greek government (Grivas had now turned against the Karamanlis and Averoff government in Greece) behind the back of a soldier who was fighting the British Empire single-handed. The Archbishop bore these attacks with forbearance and attributed them to the General's frustration in having failed in Greek politics. He himself saw a new course for Cyprus, away from the N.A.T.O. system to which Greece belonged and towards the non-aligned Afro-Asian countries. An especially clear relationship was established with President Nasser of Egypt and President Tito of Yugoslavia as leading figures among the non-aligned countries. At the same time the policy of the Archbishop was to conciliate Turkey, and he visited that country in November, 1962. All this drove the Grivas group of E.O.K.A. into a state of near fury. They could not realize that the Archbishop's tactics, as far as *enosis* and the relationships with Britain were concerned, were on the whole well advised though, perhaps, less so when it came to the perennial Turkish problem, as events were to show.

From the Turkish quarter there were from the beginning storm clouds on the horizon. The Zürich and London Agreements and the consequent Constitution of Cyprus based on them did not provide for the territorial partition of Cyprus among the Greek and Turkish communities, but provided for partition in every other sphere. The Constitution provided for election on separate rolls and gave the Turkish Vice-President of the Republic the absolute right of veto in the most important spheres of legislation, while every legislative measure had to secure separate majorities among both the Greek and Turkish Members of the Cyprus House of Representatives. In addition to this, provisions were made for the Turkish community to be heavily over-represented in the Civil Service and the armed forces of the Republic. In the sphere of Law and the Courts a system was established, under the Constitution, providing separate trials for the members of both communities by judges and courts of their own community, which revived the practice of capitulations[7] of the Ottoman Empire. Finally, all the principal towns of Cyprus were to be partitioned into Greek and Turkish municipalities.[8]

Over and above all this, Britain, as a signatory to the Treaty of Lausanne in 1923, which extinguished all Turkish rights in Cyprus, by acknowledging the right of Turkey to participate in the discussions on Cyprus went back on the Treaty of Lausanne, although legally there was no need to do so.

The first fruit of this impossible system was the failure to constitute the Cypriot army of 2,000 men as provided by the Treaties. The Treaties demanded a 60 to 40 ratio

148

of Greeks and Turks. On promptings from Ankara, the Turkish leaders demanded separate Greek and Turkish units at every level. But Makarios decided that there should be no separation at any level and this decision was vetoed by Vice-President Dr. Küchük. Makarios then decided that in that case Cyprus would not have an army at all, being a non-aligned country with limited resources under the government of an Archbishop. But the result was that secret Greek and Turkish armies began to be formed. Indeed, the Turks were discovered in this first when, in 1959, the Deniz affair occurred: the British Navy intercepted a Turkish motor-powered caique in Cypriot waters, loaded with arms and ammunition, which scuttled itself when a British boarding party went on board.

In view of the above it was fortunate that the Cyprus Constitution even got launched, the constitutional difficulties being gravely aggravated by the Deniz affair. The fact that the constitutional difficulties were settled and the President and the Vice-President of the Republic could be inaugurated was due to the military *coup d'état* in Turkey in 1960 which removed Menderes and Zorlu, who were the arch-opponents of Greek Cyprus. The new Turkish military government adopted a more conciliatory attitude, which made the Archbishop's visit to Turkey possible in 1962. However, the weakness of the military regime and the re-emergence of the former Menderes party forced the new Turkish regime to return to a traditional anti-Greek policy.

In Cyprus the stage was set for the next act of drama. Perhaps it can be said with reason that Makarios had misjudged the Turks. His background had not brought him much into contact with Turkish affairs and mentality. Perhaps he ignored the fact that the Cyprus problem was not that of *enosis* or independence but the handling of the Turkish enemy. On the surface his relations with his Turkish Vice-President were good. But there was great contrast between the two men: Archbishop Makarios beneath his hieratic Byzantine exterior is lively and witty while Dr. Küchük, on the other hand, is more stolid and taciturn. The Turks, feeling themselves the weaker party, never had their heart in the Agreements on which the Cyprus settlement was based. These Turkish suspicions made even the collection of income tax impossible, because financial Bills failed to get a majority of the Turkish votes in Parliament. It was finally this financial aspect of the situation which prompted Makarios to propose some revision of the cumbersome Constitution towards the end of 1963. Perhaps this was again an error on the part of Makarios, and, if it was, it certainly destroys the image of duplicity ascribed to him by his Turkish and British enemies. A man of duplicity would have sought to ensnare the Turks by tricks, whereas the Archbishop presented thirteen reasonable propositions which were simple in themselves and could be accepted or rejected as such.

The thirteen points submitted by Makarios to the Vice-President in November, 1963, were aimed at simplifying the Constitution, abolishing much of its dualism to make it more workable, and providing the Turkish minority in exchange with constitutional guarantees.[9] Above all, Makarios desired the abandonment of the dual municipality system, and this struck at the very root of the Turkish stand on separateness, of the Turkish community's tendency towards eventual partition. The result was a straight rejection not from Dr. Küchük but from Ankara. From Ankara also came the order to the underground Turkish forces in Cyprus to seize arms. On 24th December, 1963, the Turkish extremists in

Cyprus opened fire, thus beginning an inter-communal war which has lasted till today.

Did Makarios misjudge the situation? Was he working against impossible odds? Did he not deceive himself that the Turks and their leaders in Ankara would look on him in a charitable light? On the other hand what has happened in Cyprus was clearly the result of internal difficulties in Turkey, which began in 1960. The re-emergence of what can be called the Menderes party forced the hand of the military leaders to order violence in Cyprus, and this turn of events was very difficult to foresee owing to the execution of Menderes and Zorlu at the hands of a military junta. Also, and this must be stressed again, Makarios had been pressed to re-admit the presence of Turkey in Cyprus in London in 1959.

PART E

XIV
The Cold War comes to Cyprus

The outbreak on December 23rd, 1963, of fighting between the two communities in Cyprus was unexpected, that is to say, it was unexpected at that date, though there had been strife between the two communities ever since the events of 1958 and 1959. The Zürich and London Agreements had only patched up the situation, but bad relations continued under the veneer of constitutionalism. The fact that Makarios was taken genuinely by surprise shows that he had been too optimistic about the Turks or had overestimated his own political prestige. The only excuse that can be advanced for not foreseeing the Turkish outburst was that it was entirely spontaneous, as the Archbishop believes it to have been. This contrasts painfully with the propaganda put out by the Greek community that the Turkish outburst was the result of a long-prepared plot.

The fighting in Cyprus produced an immediate world crisis implicating Greece, Turkey and Britain and, at long range, the United States and the Soviet Union. It looked as if the Balkan-Near East kettle were going to blow up once more. Turkey and Greece were on the brink of war and Turkey, brandishing the Treaty of Guarantee, was threatening Cyprus with invasion. In these circumstances Mr. Duncan Sandys, then British Secretary for Commonwealth Relations, made a dramatic flight to Cyprus. His first task was to consolidate a ceasefire and arrange for the Greek and Turkish contingents in Cyprus to be put under British command—the British now being neutral in the struggle; true irony of fate.

In this bleak situation the position of the cold war began to crystallize: the United States and Britain were committed to Turkey through N.A.T.O.; Greece, although another member of N.A.T.O., was committed to Cyprus, which was non-aligned. In these circumstances the Soviet Union issued a serious warning against foreign intervention in Cyprus and took up its position behind both Greece and Cyprus—a traditional and classical manœuvre for Russia, made possible by the advent to power of the Papandreou government. Makarios, no doubt encouraged by this turn of events, sprang his own private bombshell. On 1st January 1964, while Mr. Sandys was still in Cyprus, the Cyprus government announced that it had abrogated the Treaty signed in London with Greece, Turkey and Britain. Makarios showed thereby that he recognised the Treaties, particularly the one with Turkey, to be the chief evil forced on him in London in 1959, as they restored in Cyprus the pre-Lausanne situation. To be fully independent of Turkey, Cyprus had to be independent of everybody, and this included not only Britain but also mother Greece. Such tearing up of international Treaties has not been unknown in recent European history. However, in the case of Cyprus, this has been done by a small and peaceful country fighting for its very existence against neo-colonialist forces extinguishing its entity. Mr. Sandys immediately descended on the Archbishop and his cabinet in session. Sandys said to Makarios: 'You can't do this.' Makarios replied calmly: 'Well, I've done it.' Sandys then said: 'If you don't retract, the Turks will be here in twenty-four hours and everyone will think they were quite within their rights. What consultations did you have before doing this?' Makarios replied: 'I've written to all heads of governments in the world.' Sandys, taken aback, asked: 'All of them, including the British government?' 'Well, not quite all. I didn't send notes to the British, Turkish and Greek governments because I thought they were all too closely involved.' Sandys retorted to this: 'You've got to eat your words, and there is no time to be lost.' The Archbishop replied to this proposition: 'I never eat my words.' 'I'm afraid you have no option and I will do my best to help you find a formula.' They then went on to produce the following piece of prose:

'In my telegrams today to heads of governments I stated that we have decided to abrogate the Treaties of Guarantee and Alliance. This may have given the impression that we had abrogated these Treaties.

'I wish to make clear that the meaning intended to be conveyed was that it is our desire to secure the termination of these Treaties by appropriate means.'

After this little exhibition, Makarios tried a face-saver by saying to Sandys: 'This was all a misunderstanding. It was the fault of the translation from the Greek. You see, the Greek word doesn't mean *abrogate* but only *desire to abrogate*.' Sandys then turned to the Cyprus Foreign Minister and asked: 'Which was the original text, the Greek or the English?' Kyprianou, obviously caught out, blushed and said: 'The English.'[1]

Sandys then worked hard to sell Makarios the idea of another London tripartite conference, but here Makarios showed his true mettle: he reverted to his stand of 1954–7. Now the cause was not *enosis* but the fact that the Cyprus Treaties had been imposed on the Cypriots by duress and, therefore, were invalid. Makarios's only desire now was to ensure recognition of the sovereign status of his government. He expected the London Conference to fail and this, he feared, would raise tensions instead of abating them. However, under the pressure of his own ministers, Makarios agreed to send representatives to the London Conference before having recourse to the United Nations. He expressed his attitude in the following words: 'I prefer to let the Conference fail slowly, rather than refuse to be represented.'[2]

The London Conference began on 15th January, 1964, with the Cypriot Turks demanding a watered-down version of partition, namely federation of the Greek majority area with a self-governing Turkish canton into which the Turkish Cypriots were to be concentrated. The Conference dragged on, as Makarios expected it to, and the leaders of both delegations were withdrawn. On their return there was no question of a compromise and the Conference became concerned with the mundane task of peace-keeping in Cyprus. A scheme was proposed to put Cyprus under N.A.T.O. jurisdiction. Makarios rejected any approach from N.A.T.O. despite the fact that President Johnson of the United States sent a high-ranking State Department official to persuade him into accepting a N.A.T.O. plan. In this he was supported by a serious warning from the Soviet Union that any attempt to bring Cyprus under N.A.T.O. control would be a threat to world peace. Indeed, the 'Green Line', the temporary cordon established in Nicosia by British troops between the Greek and Turkish communities, had become a cold-war front.

During this crisis Makarios staked out his policy: absolute sovereignty; absolute non-alignment; absolute reliance on the United Nations and the Afro-Asian anti-colonialist block in it. It was high time for a declaration as February was the worst month of the crisis. A major battle was fought between the Greeks and and Turks in Limassol and Turkey prepared an invasion fleet. Only American diplomacy (bent on excluding Russian intervention), backed by the presence of the United States Sixth Fleet, persuaded the Turks not to indulge in such a folly. The upshot of the February crisis was that Britain appealed to the Security Council, forestalling the appeal of the Government of Cyprus. Makarios's non-alignment policy then bore fruit, as Russia did not obstruct the dispatch of a peace-keeping U.N. force to Cyprus, which was a guarantee against the island coming under N.A.T.O. Another battle took place at Ktima despite the presence of British peace-keeping troops in the town. The Turks got the worst of that battle. Turkey again threatened invasion; and Greece, when the Archbishop was in Athens at the funeral of King Paul, declared she would not hesitate to fight if Turkey attempted invasion. By March 1964, together with the British contingent on the island, there was a U.N. peace-keeping force of 7,000 men and a U.N. negotiator had been appointed to solve the Cyprus tangle. In fact, however, virtual partition had come to stay in Cyprus: the Turks had eliminated themselves from the life of Cyprus and were virtually kept in concentration camps supplied by the United Nations.

The attitude of the Archbishop to the United Nations is that of extreme caution, while appreciating the political and economic value of their presence in the island and the fact that it led to a cessation of armed hostilities. Cyprus, that is Greek Cyprus, has now got its own armed forces. These forces, including the national guard, began coming into force immediately fighting began, but the staff work was the achievement of the Minister of the Interior, Mr. P. Georghadjis. These forces were, at first,

the fusion of private armies drawing on government
stocks of arms while husbanding their own. General
Grivas himself returned to Cyprus in June 1964, to
take command of the armed forces, but in reality to
make sure that Makarios should not stray too far from
the Hellenic and anti-Communist path. This is, indeed,
a problem from the Greek point of view, as the Archbishop's policy is undoubtedly now that of genuine
independence. He does not want any solution being
imposed on Cyprus, whether by N.A.T.O. or by Greece,
and he has gone to great pains to ensure that the United
Nations keeps the peace only, seeks for a solution but
is not in the position to impose this solution (if ever
found) on the people of Cyprus and its government.

In the meantime the last battle was fought in Cyprus.
The blockade of Turkish enclaves intensified military
preparations on both sides. The battle was fought in
August, 1964, at Kokkina, a small village on the north-
west coast of Cyprus, where the Turks were believed to
be landing arms from Turkey for the purpose of a
military build-up. The Greeks were attacking Kokkina,
backed by artillery and rockets, when the Turkish air-
force interfered in the battle with napalm bombs and
rockets and a Turkish invasion seemed imminent. But
by this time Makarios had become an expert in handling
international crises of this sort. He informed the Turks,
through their American friends, that an all-out offensive
was to be launched against all Turkish communities in
Cyprus if the bombing did not stop; he appealed to
the Soviet Union for help and received a promise of
immediate support if the Turks were to move. On the
other hand, the United States had already, on 5th
June, 1964, secretly warned Turkey that they could not
count on U.S. or N.A.T.O. support against the Soviet
Union if she unilaterally took action against Cyprus

which led to Soviet intervention. At the same time Makarios agreed to ease the economic blockade of the Turkish Cypriots. Makarios followed up this triumph by acquiring a shipment of heavy arms from Russia and Greece, which tipped the military balance on the island in favour of the Greeks.

The situation at the end of 1964 was that Makarios had built a solid anti-Turkish and anti-N.A.T.O. front based on Russian support as well as Egyptian, not to mention the support of the Greek Cypriot Communists and the Left in general. In these circumstances the United States government began favouring the cause of *enosis*, as union with Greece, a N.A.T.O. country, would make Cyprus a N.A.T.O. territory and eliminate the left-wing. But *enosis* was anathema to Turkey, and without Turkey there could be no N.A.T.O. in the eastern Mediterranean. The Americans advanced the Acheson Plan which envisaged the union of Cyprus with Greece, minus sovereign base areas to be held in Cyprus by Turkey instead of Britain, plus a general N.A.T.O. base in Cyprus. The plan was rejected by Makarios, who was determined to seek the backing of the United Nations Assembly for his claim to complete independence.

The end of 1964 and the beginning of 1965 saw the attempt by the Cyprus government to get a clear-cut support from the Assembly for a resolution stating the right of Cyprus to unfettered sovereignty, but owing to a dispute about financial contributions to the U.N. peace-keeping force, the Cyprus issue was not even debated. Consequently in March 1965 the new U.N. mediator, Galo Plaza, submitted his report for the solution of the Cyprus issue to the Secretary General of the United Nations.[3] The main points of the plan rejected both the right of Cyprus to union with Greece and the Turkish claim to partition. The plan was also unsatisfactory from the point of view that it advocated the complete demilitarization of the island. This plan was rejected by the Turkish government, which not only rejected the plan but Galo Plaza himself as mediator, while Makarios objected to the proposed surrender of the right to choose *enosis* and the right to maintain armed forces.

It became clear during the course of 1965 that, despite consistent attacks on Archbishop Makarios in the British press for being a tool of Greek 'expansionism', Makarios, on the contrary, was far from being a Greek puppet. Greece was committed to defend the interests of the Greek Cypriots without any comparable increase in her influence over or control of the policies of the Cyprus government. The constitutional crisis in Greece, from the overthrow of the Papandreou government in the second half of 1965 to the recent military *coup d'état*, further strengthened Makarios's hand. In December, 1965, Makarios did succeed in securing the adoption by the United Nations Assembly of a resolution which supported his claim for 'unfettered independence' for Cyprus and discounted the Turkish claim to the right of intervention based on the Zürich and London Treaties. Makarios had won his fight to establish the fact that the Treaties which fettered the sovereignty of his State and threatened it with foreign intervention were contrary to the Charter of the United Nations and therefore invalid. However, the number of abstentions was very large and Britain and the Soviet Union were among those who abstained.

After nearly three years of what can be described as the Cyprus crisis, which had become part of the cold war, Makarios had managed to establish a principle which was very different from the cause of *enosis* of which he had been at one time the principal embodiment. The new principle was that of 'unfettered independence', which meant that Cyprus alone would decide on union or *enosis*, but would not suffer *enosis* to be enforced on it. Such a subtle position is worthy of a theologian brought up in the best tradition of scholastic complexities. This, together with the ability to get on somehow with General Grivas, proves that Makarios is one of the most consummate political manipulators of modern times. This is just as well, for the affairs of Cyprus, handled with less dialectical skill, could have had a very unfortunate ending.

XV
Makarios versus the Problems of Independence

There is little doubt that the Cyprus problem has now become a part of the wider eastern Mediterranean–Middle East problem, which itself is the perennial survival of the Near Eastern problem arising from the decay of the former Ottoman Empire. The course of events in Cyprus since independence, in 1960, has been responsible for abrupt and dramatic changes in the regimes of Turkey and Greece. Already in 1960 the independence of Cyprus proved a deadly blow to the prestige of the Menderes regime in Turkey. The Republic of Cyprus with Archbishop Makarios as its President was interpreted as a success for the Greek side and a personal triumph for Makarios, who had been held up for years as a satanic arch-enemy of Turkey. The armed confrontation between Greece and Turkey, resulting from the events of 1963, was responsible for the emergence of the Papandreou government in Greece, the consequent left-wing movement in the army officers obviously dissatisfied with the American support of Turkey, which in turn, by way of reaction, led to the right-wing *coup d'état* of 1967. The resulting situation has been confusing. In Turkey the army represented forces originally to the left of the Menderes regime, but has now yielded place to a government based largely on the former Democratic party of Menderes and Bayar.[1] In

Greece the army was definitely to the right of the centre-left government of George Papandreou, which anyhow had been forced out of office by political intrigue two years before the ultimate *coup d'état*. Whether the army in Greece, in contrast with Turkey, will ultimately yield to a regime to the left of it is at present unanswerable.

The events of December, 1963, confronted Makarios with a novel challenge: he had, as President, to occupy himself with military operations. For somebody as essentially ecclesiastic and political as the Archbishop this was something alien to his nature. It was no longer a case of inspiring the struggle of an underground organization to be directed in the field by General George Grivas. Makarios was on his own and he had to face the ordeal of battle and, perhaps, a Turkish invasion. There is no doubt that the Turkish leadership in Cyprus had decided, by the end of 1963, to swing the Zürich and London Agreements towards partition, always their ultimate aim, and they had now received definite encouragement from Ankara that the time had come to settle the issue by arms.

The outburst of fighting in December, 1963, showed that the Cypriot Turks were well organized for launching their struggle. It was an open secret they were receiving arms from Turkey with this end in mind,[2] but the fact that their move took Makarios and the Cyprus government by surprise proved that armed action was unexpected. Despite the fact that the whole Turkish community flew to arms the Turks failed to seize any significant area of Cyprus in order to establish partition. The reason for this was that the Turkish community in Cyprus has never occupied any special areas of the island. The Turks in Cyprus were interspersed[3] among the Greeks all over the island. In such circumstances a successful Turkish partition of Cyprus could only have

165

been achieved by the outnumbered Cypriot Turks with the help of armed intervention from Turkey. The immediate task, therefore, of Makarios became the containment of the revolted Turkish enclaves and the prevention of a Turkish invasion. This called for a high degree of political and diplomatic skill, as it involved the whole complicated and complex structure of the Zürich and London Agreements and the juridical basis of his government. To beat back the Turkish *coup* against Cyprus would mean the *de facto* revision of the Constitution, making Cyprus a consolidated and therefore Greek-dominated state. It would also lead to the abrogation of the Treaties with Greece, Turkey and Britain,[4] which were contrary to the conception of complete sovereignty. A fully independent Greek-dominated Cyprus would then be in a good position to achieve, if it wished to, union with Greece and on its own terms, too. What was in the scales in December 1963 was either ultimate triumph or destruction and war. There is no doubt that Makarios by his skill and patience, following December 1963, by not abusing the military advantage which had accrued to the Greek side in Cyprus, has been one of the principal factors in preventing a catastrophic war between Greece and Turkey, which would only have been the traditional Balkan prelude to the rapid advent of World War Three.

It is hard to conceive of anybody but a man trained for spiritual responsibility, which is the essential factor in Makarios's background, confronting such an inflammable situation with humanity—even humility—in the face of provocations of a nature that would have inspired more conventional nationalistic leaders to take, perhaps, a very different path.

In the circumstances it is difficult to imagine that Makarios should have envisaged that the difficulties concerning the Turkish minority would end in bloodshed. It has already been observed that, unlike the heads of many newly independent states, Makarios refused to lavish any attention on providing himself with armed forces. On the contrary, he welcomed the difficulties created by the Turks over the formation of the new Republic's army, to declare that Cyprus should have no armed forces at all. This must have been the first move towards unilateral disarmament in the history of the world. He showed more preoccupation in constructing a new archiepiscopal palace, built at the cost of £300,000, and for which marbles and mosaics had been imported from Italy. In addition the palace was carpeted and furnished in the most expensive styles. However, the splendour of the new palace was to serve as an abode for the collections and archives of the Archbishopric. In addition to palace gildings Makarios, as President, devoted himself to such schemes as irrigations, roads, harbour and airport improvements.[5] He was clearly not interested in any security arrangements and left them to his Minister of the Interior. That there was just enough military organization among the Greeks in Cyprus in December 1963 to frustrate the Turkish designs was due to a number of former E.O.K.A. fighters who had rallied to the side of the Archbishop. Yet, reluctance to face the problems of violence and security, although most praiseworthy in a religious leader, is hardly a virtue in the case of a head of state. Makarios's neglect of security could have had deadly effects. Since his terrible experience of December 1963, Makarios has shown that he has been willing to learn from his mistakes and has recognized the importance of the military aspects of statesmanship, although he had to assign this task to General Grivas.[6]

It is time to ask what has been the result of the 1963

breakdown of the Republic of Cyprus. The crisis is now in its seventh year, but, on the surface, little seems to have changed. The sun still shines, the tourists come and go, the economy is booming, and on the whole things seem to be peaceful. This has been achieved, as stated above, by the presence of the U.N. peace-keeping force[7] with its green lines and Turkish zones and by the patience and good sense of the Archbishop. The policy of Makarios then seems to be to keep his head and not to yield to Turkish threats, as he demonstrated when he ignored the Turkish ultimatum in March, 1964. On the whole he is now assured that the Turks would not attempt any intervention in Cyprus as long as no *enosis* takes place and there is no massacre of the Turkish population. Makarios proceeds cautiously, consolidates the Greek hold on most of the island, and maintains diplomatic pressure at the United Nations. The objective behind such a policy is the hope that, in the course of time, the Turkish Cypriots would become worn out by the semi-siege conditions under which they are living and would return to the posts they held before the 1963 insurrection, thus enabling the affairs of the island to be run smoothly. He is, it seems, prepared to wait for many years, if necessary, in order to increase his freedom of action and to establish the *de facto* independence of Cyprus. Then, he feels, the question of *enosis* and the Turkish minority could be re-examined in a new light.

Turkey has been taken by surprise by such tactics and is not in a position to bring pressure to bear on the Greek Cypriots. All it can do is to bring pressure to bear on Greece by means of repressive measures against the Greek minority in Turkey and the position of the Ecumenical Patriarch in Constantinople, all of which proves that the territorial conflict between Greece and

Turkey has not been resolved and the Cyprus issue comes every day more to resemble the Cretan issue before the First World War.

The question remains whether the tactics favoured by Makarios are the right ones. Makarios seems to feel that time is on his side, but one could argue that this policy is, in fact, merely one of procrastination. The report of the Secretary General of the U.N., U Thant, to the Security Council on the situation in Cyprus, May 1971, refers to an increase in tension and a deterioration in the political atmosphere and gives a warning that, although the U.N. troops have kept peace on the island for the last seven years, the problems between the two communities are no nearer to a resolution and Cyprus could be facing a 'major crisis' in the near future, threatening the peace of the eastern Mediterranean. Furthermore, stalemate in Cyprus and the United Nations protection of the Turkish areas has brought about a state of virtual partition, though not the type that the Turks desired. Instead of an area of the island being ceded outright to Turkey or constituted as a sovereign Turkish Cypriot area in a federated Cyprus, the Turkish Cypriots, who have rebelled against the Republic of Cyprus, hold a few scattered areas all over the island. These areas are supplied from Turkey by means of the United Nations peace-keeping force. These Turkish-held areas already constitute a *de facto* state within a state. Any moment now Turkey may proclaim them to be annexed to the Republic of Turkey or they can proclaim themselves as a separate Cypriot Turkish state to be recognized as such by Turkey and some other countries. What would then be the move which Makarios could make? The original Constitution had excluded partition or any fragmentation of Cyprus and, therefore, under it such a move would be illegal. But the original Constitution, and the Agreements on which it was based, have been repudiated. This state of affairs, which has also been brought about by the secession of the Turkish Vice-President, the Turkish Ministers and the Turkish Members of Parliament, has thrown doubts on the continued legality of the Archbishop's government. It is fortunate that, for international reasons, this point has not been pressed home. Although neither Britain nor Turkey has recognized the unilateral abrogation of the Treaties of 1959, the Archbishop's government continues to be recognized by the United Nations as the only Government of Cyprus and most countries, including Britain, maintain diplomatic relations with the Archbishop's government. This is precisely the *de facto* state of affairs which Makarios seems to perpetuate through the passage of time. Whether he will succeed or not depends largely on the neat balance between Greece and Turkey.

The question of *enosis* still underlines the Cyprus issue although there has been a curious reversal of parts in this drama. Originally the desire for *enosis* came from Cyprus and enabled Makarios to climb to the top as its standard bearer. Latterly, it must be honestly acknowledged, there has been an abatement of irredentist passions in Greece since 1960, and Makarios has been both unable and unwilling to stir them up by assuming the mantle of Venizelos. This is the result of Turkish pressure exerted against Greece to extract from her a price for Cyprus which she could hardly afford to pay. This, in turn, might encourage a government in Athens to settle the whole problem at a price which it then would try to extract from Cyprus. The conditions, therefore, of union with Greece under such circumstances do not seem as easy as they did 10 years ago. Moreover, there is just the possibility that the Archbishop and his ministers prefer to be the government of an independent Cyprus or at least a separate Cyprus rather than to hand over their homeland to Athens and retire from the lime-light. This accusation has been levelled against Makarios by his adversaries in Cyprus, in Greece and in Britain, although it is difficult in the present situation to come to any definite conclusion. In changed circumstances, only the Archbishop and his God know what his policy would be in this respect.

It is certain that whatever plans the Archbishop had, have been upset by the 1967 *coup d'état* in Greece. There is no doubt that Makarios could, somehow, get on with the late George Papandreou and that he himself had always occupied a left-of-centre position in politics, which is not an unusual thing among churchmen-politicians. He has certainly laboured to establish good relations with the Soviet Union and other east European States as well as with the Greek Cypriot left-wing. As befits his office, Makarios has never been a professional anti-Communist as this would have conflicted with his concept of simple patriotism and devotion to the national idea. He also realizes, as events have proved, that Soviet support is necessary to neutralize Turkish threats. With a right-wing government in Athens the prospect of *enosis* looks hardly bright for the Cypriots who have inherited, when all is said and done, a liking for British liberalism linked to Parliamentary traditions. Such a situation has made all left-of-centre Cypriots less than enthusiastic for the spread of the mainland regime to their country, which would also be accompanied by the withdrawal of Cyprus from the Commonwealth, which contributes to the economic stability of the island. Makarios has, in fact, achieved a unique position in the Hellenic world: he is the only democratically elected leader still in office.

He has remained loyal to King Constantine and is a pressing influence for his return to Greece and the resolution of the constitutional question in Greece in a liberal sense.

The whole policy of Makarios as President of Cyprus could really be described by the formula of 'wait and see'. But time, as the saying goes, waits for no one. The waiting policy of Makarios has, indicated above, led to the entrenchment of virtually sovereign Turkish areas. It has also led to impatience and strains and stresses in the Greek camp. Makarios's divided position as President and spiritual leader has imposed on him an indecisively tolerant attitude even towards his enemies. Perhaps his deep Christian faith makes him offer the other cheek too much. Characteristically, he has been extremely slack in matters concerning his personal security which has been responsible for a dramatic and almost successful assassination attempt on 5th March, 1970. He escaped death almost by a miracle. This attack, it is believed, had been carried out by a dissident group frustrated by Makarios's waiting policy and alleged back-pedalling on *enosis*.

The assassination attempt has been up-to-date the most grievous blow that Makarios has received, in his own estimation. Broadcasting to the people of Cyprus after the event he spoke from the depth of his soul when he said: 'But if the bullets did not also strike my body, they struck and wounded my soul. And I feel really the deepest pain because there have been Greek Cypriots, acting on their own, or as agents of others, who have dared such an attempt, turning their weapons on me and shooting at me with murderous bullets.'[8] These words show the bitterness of Makarios at the ingratitude of even a small and irresponsible section of his people. He continued: 'My soul is full of sorrow for this murderous attempt, for the act itself, for the circumstances under which the act was performed, for the fact that even a few men have performed it without hesitation.'

Typically he ended his address with Christian forgiveness: 'For those who have attempted to take away my life, I pray to God to forgive them.'

Ever since the attempt on his life Makarios has felt that he has been accompanied by the shadow of death. It is to be hoped that in the depth of his depression he might come to re-examine some aspects of his policy and perhaps realize that some aspects of it have been frustrating and deeply wounding for some who have suffered as much as he for the cause of Cyprus. Particularly as it looked at one time, as if the assassination attempt was going to unchain a whole new wave of bloody violence and undermine the unity and authority of the State.[9]

Makarios has often been the target of criticism that he is too fond of his office as President and with his own position in Cyprus to the detriment of his ecclesiastical functions. Recently Makarios has taken steps to nail such criticisms. He has engaged in considerable missionary enterprise in Africa where he made a historical journey to Kenya. This journey had nothing to do with politics. It was concerned with the establishment of an outpost of the Orthodox Church and a Seminary School in Black Africa, south of the Sahara, where the field had been left almost exclusively open to the Roman Catholic and Protestant churches. Needless to say the Seminary is going to be financed by the Orthodox Church of Cyprus. During his visit he administered collective baptism to some 5,000 African converts. The historical significance of these activities lies in the fact that it is a resumption of the missionary ambitions, in that part of Africa, of another Byzantine ruler, the Emperor

Justinian in the 6th century. Of equal religious and
political significance is the invitation extended to
Makarios by the Soviet Union to pay a State visit in
June, 1971, and to be present at the enthronement of
the new Russian Orthodox Patriarch.

In the meantime Makarios occupies a position of
lonely eminence in Nicosia. His life is simple and
divided between the cares of his office and his religious
duties. Many times he has expressed the desire to devote
himself entirely to his religious office once all dangers
are passed. He may also give thought to a curious trick
of fate whereby Britain, his early enemy and opponent of
enosis, has been largely eliminated from the problem.
The cause of *enosis*, of which he has been the most
distinguished champion, now depends entirely on the
workings of the balance of power within the context of
the cold war and on the political future of Greece. There
is no doubt that Makarios has shown a great degree of
fortitude and dignity in the face of adversity. His name
will be forever linked with the history of Cyprus in the
20th century. His qualities are derived from his faith
and general background and both are responsible for
his impressive dignity. It is hardly conceivable that
anybody without his dignity and strength of conviction
could have inspired the cause of *enosis* and Cypriot
independence with such fervour; he has certainly been
its best representative. The future might hold for
Makarios and Cyprus great triumphs or, conversely,
great ordeals. But whatever he is obliged to face he will
at all times maintain his hieratic calm and dignified
bearing so reminiscent of a Byzantine icon of the great
age. He incorporates the greatness and resilience of the
Greek Orthodox Church and its unbroken tradition.
That Church, too, has managed to survive triumphs and
adversities because it believed in the ultimate triumph

of spiritual values. Makarios faces the future with assurance strengthened by the spiritual values which he represents and serves. But whatever the outcome, he has served Cyprus and her people well.

Conclusion

The unique position of Makarios as the only churchman who is head of State has already been dealt with. In the absence of any other form of political life only the elected Archbishops could be the store of the political authority and experience. However, now that Cyprus is an independent Republic with a constitutional regime there is no absolute necessity why the next head of State should be an Archbishop. The contemporary political climate dictates that a successor to Makarios as President of Cyprus should be a layman. Such a development would naturally sever the union between Church and State which is exemplified by the Archbishop-President. Nevertheless, if Cyprus is going to remain an independent Republic, the elected lay President will be confronted by a popularly-elected Archbishop. This state of affairs could lead to grave friction between Church and State, to the neutralization of the political authority of both leaders. Since it is inconceivable that the President of Cyprus should be elected in any other way than by popular vote, it would seen imperative that in these circumstances, with the Archbishops of Cyprus playing an exclusively ecclesiastical role, the Church of Cyprus should alter the mode of election of its head and transfer it exclusively to the clergy. Only then the people of Cyprus would be spared the danger of having two heads

M

both popularly elected and claiming full democratic powers accruing from this fact.

The problem of the Turkish minority as it arose after 1963 has not been treated extensively in this book, as it did not form an integral part of Makarios's struggle for the freedom of Cyprus before independence. The Turkish problem has been a problem of Cyprus independence. It has been handled since 1963 by the great powers, both inside and outside the United Nations, and by direct negotiations between Greece and Turkey. It is obvious that, under the existing legal and political circumstances, Makarios is unable to offer his own solution to this problem without the agreement of the powers concerned. The problem continues to remain unsolved, although the presence of the U.N. initially took much heat out of the situation.

A contingent of British troops forms part of the United Nations force. However, following U Thant's warning of the prospect of an 'apparently indefinite commitment for the United Nations in Cyprus' (Report to the Security Council, May 1971), Britain has announced her decision to place a limit on the financial contribution that she has been making over the past seven years.

In addition to British Army units, which are a part of the United Nations peace-keeping force, there are two British bases on Cyprus, over which Britain has sovereign rights, which were negotiated by a Treaty signed between Britain and Cyprus in 1960. Of course, British servicemen of all the three armed services on the bases come under direct British command and have nothing to do with the U.N. peace-keeping force. In addition it must be stressed that the British forces in Cyprus are not integrated into N.A.T.O. They can only be used by Britain for exclusively British purposes. This point has been the condition for Makarios's acceptance of the Treaty establishing these bases because of his avowed policy of non-alignment of Cyprus in the cold war.

It now seems certain that the crowning achievement of Makarios's career will not be so much the independence of Cyprus as the solution of the Cyprus question, which is the problem of the Turkish minority. In November 1963 Makarios made his now famous proposals to amend the Cyprus Constitution,[1] which had been imposed on the island without much thought as to its workability. The eminent British jurist Professor de Smith, Professor of Public Law at the University of London, has described the Constitution of Cyprus as 'probably the most rigid in the world. It is certainly the most detailed and (with the possible exception of Kenya's new Constitution) the most complicated. It is weighed down by checks and balances, procedural and substantive safeguards, guarantees and prohibitions. Constitutionalism has run riot in harness with Communalism. The government of the Republic must be carried on but never have the chosen representatives of a political majority been set so daunting an obstacle course by the Constitution makers.'[2] The gist of Makarios's thirteen proposals was to make the Constitution more workable by ironing out some of its communalistic contradictions. The Turkish minority would not have been deprived, by these changes, of the safeguards provided for them by the Treaty of Guarantee. However, it seems that both the Turkish minority in Cyprus and the Turkish government in Ankara suffer from a chronic fear of the Greek majority on the island despite the provisions of the Treaty of Guarantee.

Since November 1963 they have, in fact, repudiated the Zürich Agreement and the Treaty of Guarantee and have been demanding the partition of the island. Quite apart from the fact that partition has not worked very well where it has been applied (Korea, Vietnam, Ireland, etc.), it has become abundantly obvious that the Greek majority in Cyprus will never agree to the partition of their small island, and this is now the chief political creed of the Greek population in place of former *enosis*; if any solution of the Turkish minority problem can be found, it must not include partition or impair the right of the majority.

The question may be asked: what is the solution to the problem of the Turkish minority in Cyprus? The plain answer to this is that for reasons well-evidenced since November, 1963, the unity of both the island and the Constitution must be respected and preserved by all means. On the other hand, the fears of the Turkish minority must be quenched as far as possible by the grant of the widest possible sphere of, first of all, cultural and religious autonomy. This autonomy of the Turkish minority, as well as other rights already held under the Constitution of Cyprus, should be embodied in a Treaty directly negotiated between Cyprus and Turkey, which, however, would not impair the sovereignty of Cyprus as the Treaty of Guarantee of 1960 did. Such a Treaty, moreover, like other treaties of a similar nature should then be registered with, and guaranteed by, the U.N. The author has good reasons to believe that such a solution would be most welcome to both Archbishop Makarios and the Turkish government in Ankara. It is the leaders of the Turkish minority in Cyprus who are trying to maintain their stand on partition by injecting into the unitary status of the island, now agreed upon, the idea of 'cantonization'. Cantonization would simply bring back partition by the back door, without any of its political and administrative advantages, by dividing Cyprus into separate Greek and Turkish enclosures which would encourage communal separatism and strife and lead back directly to the events of December 1963. It is for the Ankara government to make good sense prevail with the Turkish leaders in Cyprus. In 1965, the chief spokesman for the Turkish community, Raouf Denktash, entered into a dialogue—which is still going on at the present time—with Glafkos Clerides, representative of the Greek side, aiming at a peaceful solution of the island's problems. Unfortunately, according to the May 1971 report of the U.N. Secretary General, there had been a marked lack of progress in these intercommunal talks. Without the goodwill of the leaders of the Turkish community of Cyprus, Makarios's hands are tied. This would be a cruel paradox as it has been shown by events that his attitude to the Turkish minority has been more moderate than any other leader of the Greek Cypriots. It would be tragic, indeed, if no solution to the problem of the Turkish minority is produced while Makarios is President. Because he alone, at present, has the strength and stature to guarantee the success of any such solution.

Bibliography

1 Alastos, D., *Cyprus in History*, London, 1955.
2 Alastos, D., *Cyprus Guerrilla*, London, 1960.
3 Cobham, C. D., *Excerpta Cypria*, C.U.P., 1908.
4 Dixon, H., *British Cyprus*, London, 1879.
5 Foley, Charles, *Island in Revolt*, London, 1962.
6 Foley, Charles, *Legacy of Strife*, London, 1964.
7 *Greek Communal Chamber, A Handbook on the Island's Past and Present*, Nicosia, 1964.
8 Grivas, G., *Memoirs*, edited by Charles Foley, London, 1964.
9 Hill, G. (Sir), *A History of Cyprus*, C.U.P., 1940–52.
10 Home, G., *Cyprus: Then and Now*, London, 1960.
11 Le Geyt, Captain P. S., *Makarios in Exile*, Nicosia, 1961.
12 Luke, H. (Sir), *Cyprus: A Portrait and an Appreciation*, London, 1957.
13 Mayer, P., *Cyprus and Makarios*, London, 1960.
14 Newman, P., *A Short History of Cyprus*, London, 1953.
15 Stephens, R., *Cyprus, a Place of Arms*, London, 1966.
16 Storrs, R. (Sir), *Orientations*, London, 1937.
17 Storrs, R. (Sir), and O'Brien, B. J., *The Handbook of Cyprus*, London, 1930.
18 Turner, W., *A Journal of a Tour in the Levant*, London, 1820.

19 Vanezis, P. N., *The Present-day World Position of English and its Importance for Communication and General Advancement*, Ph.D. thesis, London University, 1967.

Appendix

POPULATION SINCE THE MIDDLE AGES[1]

Year	Total estimated population	Remarks
Early 14th century	400,000	Estimate based on 1491 figure.
1491	168,000	Venetian count in *Mas Latrie*, vol. III, 147,000, about 20,000 persons not included.
1540	217,000	Venetian count (Attar), 197,000, about 20,000 persons not included.
1571	290,000	Turkish count, 85,000 Christian tax-payers, plus dependents, plus 20,000 Turks.
1641	130,000	Turkish count, 25,000 tax-payers, plus dependents, plus Turks.
1670	100,000	Turkish count, 15,000 tax-payers, plus dependents, plus Turks.

Year	Total estimated population	Remarks
1745	85,000	Turkish count, 12,000 tax-payers, plus dependents, and 4,000 Turkish families.
1767	80,000	Turkish count, of villages only, approximately 10,000 tax-payers, plus dependents and 6,000 Turkish families.
1777	100,000	Estimate of Kyprianos (37,000 Christians, 47,000 Moslems)—Christians probably understated.
1821	110,000	Estimate of Trikoupi (21,000 each Christians and Moslems, plus dependents).
1881	186,000	First census under British occupation (140,000 Christians, 45,500 Moslems).
1911	274,000	Fourth census (218,000 Christians, 45,000 Moslems).
1946	450,000	Seventh census (369,500 Christians, 80,500 Moslems).
1959	561,000	Cyprus: Colonial Report, 1959, p. 16. Greek Cypriots (78·8 per cent) and Turkish Cypriots (17·5 per cent): other minorities.
1960	573,566	Out of a total of 573,566 inhabitants, 441,656 or 77 per cent were Greeks,

Year	Total estimated population	Remarks
1969	621,990	104,942 or 18·3 per cent were Turks and 26,968 or 4·7 per cent were other minorities. Out of these 113,204 or 18·2 per cent are Turks and 479,562 are Greeks and 29,224 are other minorities.

A SUMMARY OF THE ZÜRICH AND LONDON AGREEMENTS

The Constitution of the Republic of Cyprus of the 16th August, 1960, was based on the two agreements reached in Zürich and London.

The Constitution was put into force on the 16th August, 1960, when the Republic of Cyprus was established, without being voted for either by the people of Cyprus directly or by its duly elected representatives, for this purpose, in a constituent assembly.

At the same time when the Constitution was signed and came into force the following three international treaties were signed and put into force: the Treaty of Establishment, between Cyprus, Britain, Greece and Turkey, to establish the independent Republic of Cyprus; the Treaty of Guarantee, between Cyprus, Britain, Greece and Turkey, to put the Constitution into effect; the Treaty of Alliance, between Cyprus, Greece and Turkey, to protect the Constitution.

The last two aforementioned Treaties were given constitutional force (Article 181 of the Constitution) and were annexed to the Constitution as Annexes I and II.

The Republic of Cyprus, established on the 16th August, 1960, came to have a Greek President elected by the Greeks and a Turkish Vice-President elected by the Turks. The Vice-President was granted the right of a final veto on any law of the House of Representatives and on any decision of the Council of Ministers concerning foreign affairs, defence and security. The Council of Ministers was composed of 10 Ministers, three of whom had to be Turks and were nominated for appointment by the Vice-President.

In the House of Representatives, the Turks, though less than 20 per cent of the population, were granted 30 per cent of the seats and their Representatives elected separately by their co-racialists. The House could not modify the Constitution ever or at all, in so far as it concerned its basic articles, and any other modification was to require a separate majority comprising two-thirds of the Greek members and two-thirds of the Turkish members. Any modification of the electoral law, the adoption of any law relating to municipalities, and any law imposing duties or taxes was to require separate simple majorities of the Greek and Turkish members of the House.

The highest judicial organs, the Supreme Constitutional Court and the High Court of Justice, were to be presided over by neutral Presidents, being neither Greeks nor Turks, who by casting vote were to hold the balance between the Greek and Turkish members of the said courts. Whereas under the colonial regime Greek and Turkish judges, without any complaint whatsoever ever having been made, had tried all cases irrespective of the community of the litigants, it was now provided that the disputes among Turks were to be tried by Turkish judges only, disputes among Greeks by Greek judges only, and disputes between Greeks and Turks by mixed courts composed both of Greek and Turkish judges.

All the above safeguards were provided for, notwithstanding the fact that, through other clauses in the Treaty of Guarantee, the Turks had already been granted complete autonomy, legislative and administrative, in relation to educational, religious, cultural, sporting and charitable matters, co-operative and credit societies, and questions of personal status.

The Turks were also given 30 per cent of all posts in the Civil Service and the Security Forces and 40 per cent in the army, in great disproportion to their numerical strength as a minority.

Separate municipalities were provided for Greeks and Turks in the five largest towns of the island.

PRESIDENT MAKARIOS'S PROPOSALS TO AMEND THE CYPRUS CONSTITUTION

1 The right of veto of the President and the Vice-President of the Republic to be abandoned.
2 The Vice-President of the Republic to deputize for the President of the Republic in case of his temporary absence or incapacity to perform his duties.
3 The Greek President of the House of Representatives and the Turkish Vice-President to be elected by the House as a whole and not, as at present, the President by the Greek Members of the House.

4 The Vice-President of the House of Representatives to deputize for the President of the House in case of his temporary absence or incapacity to perform his duties.

5 The constitutional provisions regarding separate majorities for enactment of certain laws by the House of Representatives to be abolished.

6 Unified Municipalities to be established.

7 The administration of justice to be unified.

8 The division of the Security Forces into Police and Gendarmerie to be abolished.

9 The numerical strength of the Security Forces and of the Defence Forces to be determined by a Law.

10 The proportion of the participation of Greek and Turkish Cypriots in the composition of the Public Service and the Forces of the Republic to be modified in proportion to the ratio of the population of Greek and Turkish Cypriots.

11 The number of Members of the Public Service Commission to be reduced from ten to five.

12 All decisions of the Public Service Commission to be taken by simple majority.

13 The Greek Communal Chamber to be abolished.

GALO PLAZA REPORT SUBMITTED ON 26th MARCH 1965

The main points are:
1 Cyprus should remain an independent state and should voluntarily renounce its right to choose union with Greece.

2 The island should be demilitarized, the question of the British sovereign bases being left aside for further consideration.

3 There should be no partition or physical separation of the Greek and Turkish communities, but Turkish Cypriot rights should be guaranteed by the United Nations and supervised by a United Nations Commissioner in the island.

4 A settlement must depend in the first place on the agreement between the people of Cyprus themselves and talks should take place between the Greek and Turkish Cypriots.

Notes

Preface
1 The last time a bishop held the office of Lord Chancellor in England was in the 17th century.

Chapter I
1 Zeno established his school in a colonnade called the Stoa Poikile at Athens.

Chapter II
1 *Orientations,* Sir R. Storrs, p. 550, London, 1937.
2 The poverty and squalor of the Turkish population of Cyprus, although they arrived as conquerors, has been due to the fact that they have remained entirely agricultural, leaving all other trades, activities and, above all, commerce in the hands of the Greeks (as elsewhere in the Ottoman Empire).
3 Turkish Cypriots form 18 per cent of the population of Cyprus. For population chart see Appendix.

Chapter III
1 The Church of Greece was, until Greek independence, directly under Constantinople.
2 *Cyprus: A Portrait and an Appreciation,* Sir H. Luke, p. 77, G. G. Harrap & Co., 1957.
3 *Journal of a Tour in the Levant,* William Turner, London, 1820.
4 *Voyages d'Ali Bey el Abbassi en Afrique et en Asie,* 3 vols., Paris, 1814. Extract in Cobham, *Exce Cypria.*
5 Sir H. Luke, op. cit., p. 80.
6 *A Short History of Cyprus,* P. Newman, p. 114, Longmans, 1953.
7 Sir H. Luke, op. cit., p. 177.

NOTES

Chapter IV

1 *British Cyprus*, Hepworth Dixon, p. 139, Chapman & Hall, 1879.

Chapter V

1 *Cyprus in History*, D. Alastos, p. 308, Zeno Publishers, London, 1955.
2 Ibid., p. 308.

Chapter VI

1 For the history of the Episcopal question see Alastos, op. cit., pp. 332–3.
2 Alastos, op. cit., p. 334.
3 A letter addressed to the Cypriot Mission then in London by the Prime Minister, Lloyd George, on 14th November, 1919.
4 Alastos, op. cit., p. 345.

Chapter VII

1 Italian policy in the Dodecannese consisted in the systematic suppression of all Greek national features and the Greek language.

Chapter VIII

1 *The Memoirs of General Grivas*, edit. Charles Foley, p. 17, Longmans, January, 1964.
2 *Cyprus, A Place of Arms*, R. Stephens, p. 135, Pall Mall, 1966.
3 *Hansard*, 28th July, 1954, vol. 508.
4 *Cyprus and Makarios*, S. Mayes, p. 127, London, 1960.
5 *Memoirs*, pp. 22–3.

Chapter IX

1 National Organization for Cypriot Struggle.
2 *Full Circle*, Anthony Eden, p. 400, Cassell, 1960.
3 *Cyprus: The Dispute and the Settlement*, Chatham House, Memoranda, pp. 17–18, O.U.P., 1959.
4 *Memoirs*, p. 41.
5 Progressive Party of the Working People.

Chapter X

1 *Makarios in Exile*, P. S. Le Geyt, p. 108, Nicosia, 1961.

2 The Archbishop is known to be highly critical of the lack of adequate table manners of some of his highest civil servants and especially diplomats.

3 Le Geyt, op. cit., p. 59.

Chapter XI

1 *Treaties on Politics*, Ch. 1, par. 1.

2 *Legacy of Strife*, Charles Foley, p. 50, London, 1964.

3 Chatham House, op. cit., p. 23.

4 *Memoirs*, p. 106.

5 Though once organized he proved himself not too adverse from profiting from its activities.

6 Charles Foley, op. cit., p. 61.

7 Alastos, op. cit., p. 146.

8 Chatham House, op. cit., p. 34.

9 Charles Foley, op. cit., pp. 858 and 898.

10 When Makarios was leaving for New York, Washington announced that neither President Eisenhower nor Mr. Foster Dulles, Secretary of State, would receive him (Grivas, *Memoirs*, p. 123).

11 Charles Foley, op. cit., p. 103.

12 *Memoirs*, p. 134.

13 Chatham House, op. cit., pp. 46–7.

Chapter XII

1 *Memoirs*, p. 162.

2 *Memoirs*, p. 163.

3 Charles Foley, op. cit., p. 133.

4 Robert Stephens, op. cit., p. 165.

5 For summary of terms of Zürich and London Agreements see Appendix.

6 Robert Stephens, op. cit., pp. 165–6.

Chapter XIII

1 Charles Foley, op. cit., p. 151

2 *Memoirs*, p. 198.

3 Charles Foley, op. cit., p. 153.

4 Charles Foley, op. cit., p. 155.

5 Under the Constitution of Cyprus the President was elected by the Greek voters alone, while the Turkish Vice-President was elected on a separate Turkish electoral roll.

6 Hence the necessity of Colonel Grivas, the perfect revolutionary.
7 System whereby the Ottoman Sultans granted the right to foreigners in the former Ottoman Empire to be tried by judges of their own race and faith, i.e. their consuls.
8 This was highly impractical, owing to the comparative poverty of the Turkish community.
9 For the proposed thirteen points, see Appendix.

Chapter XIV

1 Robert Stephens, op. cit., pp. 185–6.
2 Robert Stephens, op. cit., p. 187.
3 See Appendix.

Chapter XV

1 Removed by army pressure in March 1971, which again brought into power supporters of Inonu's Republican Party.
2 The regular Greek and Turkish Army contingents stationed on the island were a plentiful source of supply for both sides.
3 There is no compact geographical Turkish area, or any area inhabited predominantly by Turks. The proportion of land ownership between Greeks and Turks is
   (a) by area, 82·9 per cent Greeks, 17·6 per cent Turks,
   (b) by value, 86·8 per cent Greeks, 13·2 per cent Turks.
4 Excluding, of course, the agreement on British sovereign bases in Cyprus.
5 The Turkish troubles in Cyprus have not interfered with the rapid economic progress of the Greek community.
6 By the middle of June, 1964, Grivas arrived in Cyprus from Athens to take a hand in the organization and training of the new Cyprus National Guard.
7 On March 14th, 1964, the Canadian Advance Guard of the U.N. Force flew into Cyprus. They were followed by others making up a peace force of nearly 7,000 men.
8 *Cyprus Bulletin*, Nicosia, 15th March, 1970, Vol. VII, No. 10, p. 3.
9 The assassination attempt was followed in a few days by the successful assassination, under mysterious circumstances, of Polycarpos Georghadjis, the former Minister of the Interior, but latterly an opponent of Makarios's policy.

Conclusion
  1 See Appendix.
  2 *The Cyprus Question*, P.I.O., p. 4, Nicosia, Cyprus, 1969.

Appendix
  1 *Cyprus: Census of Population and Agriculture 1946.* Published on
    behalf of the Government of Cyprus by the Crown Agents for
    the Colonies, 1949.

Printed in Great Britain
by The Anchor Press Ltd.,
Tiptree, Essex